B.R. AMBEDKAR
His Relevance Today

B.R. AMBEDKAR
His Relevance Today

Editors

J.S. NARAYAN RAO;

A. SOMASEKHAR;

K. AUDISESHAIAH

GYAN PUBLISHING HOUSE

NEW DELHI-110 002

B.R. AMBEDKAR: HIS REVEVANCE TODAY

ISB : 8N1-212-0439-9

ISBN: 81-212-0493-3

Published in 2013 in India by
Gyan Publishing House
23, Main Ansari Road, Daryaganj,
New Delhi - 110002
Phones : 23282060, 23261060
Fax : (011) 23285914
E-mail : books@gyanbooks.com
Website: gyanbooks.com

Printed at: G.Printers, Delhi

Foreword

Bharat Ratna Dr. B.R. Ambedkar's life reads like a great saga. Born in a humble 'untouchable' family, facing many vicissitudes of life, through dint of hard work and merit, he rose to be one of the foremost leaders and a great savant of the country, in an era of titans. His life's mission was emancipation of the downtrodden from millinnia of servitude and indigence, which is a great blot on the Indian society. Today, Babasaheb's life, ideas and ideals hold beacon light of hope and inspiration to the millions of the country. His birth centenary is an occasion to pay our humble regards to the great leader and rededicate ourselves to his ideals.

The plan of this seminar and the volume came to me through Sri K. Audiseshaiah, Director, and the Seminar Director Prof. J.S. Narayan Rao, and I am happy to find my colleagues from Osmania University among the distinguished contributors of the papers. It is always pleasing for me to encounter academic and social activism of my colleagues and others. For none can be insulated against social currents and cross-current. We physical scientists recognise society too as a great Lab.

The papers are by eminent persons like Sri V.H. Desai, professor Mumtaz Ali Khan and others and they are on a variety of topics: Babasaheb's personality, minorities, education, social upliftment, socio-economic conditions of SCs. Ambedkar & Labour and women, quality of life of SCs, Constitution and Ambedkarism, a new coinage, it seems.The authors are to be congratulated on their neat turn-outs. They speak of the great breadth of Dr. Ambedkar's ideas which are relevant not only for the present times but also for many generations to come. Dr. Ambedkar was in the nature of a great historical personality whose ideas will move millions for ages to come. For us from the field of education Dr. Ambedkar's enthroning of learning and wisdom over and above all is a lasting message.

The Institute for Social Research & Action (ISRA) and Scheduled Castes Research & Training Institute (SCR & TI), Social Welfare Department, Government of Andhra Pradesh, need to be appreciated in organising the seminar and bringing out this volume.

Hope, the volume will do their bit in making familiar to the people the many faceted contributions of the great savant who strode the Indian scene like a colossus among the giants of his times.

T. NAVANEETH RAO
Former Vice-chancellor
Osmania University
Hyderabad

Preface

We are happy to present this volume of papers of the seminar on "Relevance of Dr. B.R. Ambedkar for the Present Times", organised, jointly, by the Institute for social Research & Action (ISRA), Hyderabad, and Scheduled Cates Research & Training Institute (SCR & TI), Social Welfare Department, Government of Andhra Pradesh, Hyderabad, on 19 April, 1992 on the occasion of the birth-centenary of Babasaheb, reverence. We are grateful to the contributors of the volume for their writings. The contributions, in their own way, bring out some of the many contributions of the doctor saheb, which are of lasting value, and also throw some light on the socio-economic conditions of the SCs where much is desired to be done. Let us on the occasion, rededicate ourselves to bring cheers into the still drab lives of our SC kith and kin.

ISRA is devoted to the problems and prospects of the disadvantages. We are one with them in their downs. Andhra Pradesh Social Welfare Departments's concern is also same and more.

The idea of the seminar and the volume was initiated by ISRA, and joined by the SCR & TI. We are thankful to the then vice-chancellor of Osmania University. Prof.T. Navaneeth Rao, for evincing interest in our project and making initial contribution through the ICSSR, Southern Regional Centre (SRC), Osmania University, and also for contributing Foreword to this volume. We acknowledge the gracious help extended by the then Hon. Director, ICSSR, SRC, OU, Prof. E.G. Parameshwaran, and Deputy Director, Dr. Masood Ali Khan. We sincerely feel that the ICSSR should raise its contributions to voluntary people like us to relieve from the hassels of organising ventures like this.

Our grateful thanks to Hon'ble Smt. M. Lakshmi Devi, Minister for Social Welfare, Government of Andhra Pradesh, Sri. V. Govindrajan, IAS, Secretary to Government of Andhra Pradesh, Social Welfare Department, Sri. P. Kamaleswar Rao, IAS, Commissioner, Social Welfare, Dr. Somasekhar, Director, SCR & TI, among the finest government functionaries to come across and work with, for substantial funding and all other ready help and cooperation. We owe additional thanks to Sri. V. Govindarajan for kindly inaugurating the seminar inspite of his tight every day schedule to work. Our heartfelt thanks to Sri. M.V.P.C. Sastry, M.D., APSCCFC, for his advices.

Our gratitude to Prof. R.V.R. Chandrasekhara Rao, Vice-chancellor, Dr. B.R. Ambedkar's open university is immense for all his kindness, advice and help in all matters, and in this case for note address. We are grateful to Sri C.N. Shastry, IAS (Retd.) for his help. The Seminar and the volume could not have been a success without the dynamism of Sri K. Audiseshaiah, Director, ISRA our grateful thanks to him.

We thank Shiv Kumar, Sirish Kumar, Ahmed Sharief, S.R. Balkrishna, B. Sampath Rao, ISRA Staff, for their help. My special thanks are to Miss Y. Pushpalatha, Sri B.N. Vinoda Rao, Lecturer in Economics, New Govt. College, Malakpet, Hyderabad my Ph. D. Schalers, Deptt. of Economics, Osmania University, Hyderabad for giving me a helping hand.

Last but not the least, we are grateful to the authorities of the University of Hyderabad, especially Dr. K. Ravichandra. My Osmanian colleague, Director, Academic Staff College, University of Hyderabad, for providing their beautiful, historic Golden-threshold for the seminar.

It is our earnest desire that this volume's Notes will further spread the great personality and noble thoughts of the doctor saheb.

J.S. NARAYAN RAO

Contents

Relevance of Dr. Ambedkar Today

V. H. Desai[*]

To write on the life and work of Dr. Bhimrao Ramji Ambedkar (April 14, 1891 - Dec., 5-6, 1956) is rather an Herculean task for any writer; more so the writers who have not known this giant among giants, the great among the greats; and a luminary among the luminaries.

To me, Dr. Ambedkar was more than an institution. He had had been described by many in many ways—a social reformer, a redeemer, the law-maker and what not ? Today, when we look back and compare our notes of the happenings of yester-years and today's we rarely look to him in a national perspective.

Dr. Ambedkar was born with no silver-spoon in his mouth, yet he could attain the stature on par with the greatest men of his time. This alone should speak volumes about his personality.

'Bhim' who was the 14th child of his parents always took pride in himself that he was born to beat others. Hence 'Bhim' had to fight his way literally up the ladder and when he boasted that he was *'Chavdasa Ratna'*, he meant it and proved as such.

The excellent academic record of Ambedkar was a testimony to his intellectual brilliance.

After Graduation in 1912, he went to USA on a Baroda State Scholarship. He joined Columbia University from where he secured M.A., in Economics and Ph.D. subsequently. He went to England and joined School of Economics and Political Science, but he could not pursue his studies due to non-continuation of

---

* Hon'. Principal Bhavan's College of Communication and Management, Hyderabad; Executive-President, The Forum for Human Resource Development, Hyderabad, India, and President, The Hyderabad Freedom Fighters' Forum, Hyderabad.

scholarship. He returned to India and started teaching at Sydenham College at Bombay as professor of Economics. After saving some money from his teaching and with some financial support from his friends he went to England again to complete his studies. He did his M.Sc., in 1921 and was awarded the D.Sc., in 1923. In the same year he was also called to the Bar. All this he could achieve with a single-minded devotion. He fought all his way to achieve excellence in whatever he did.

In the year 1924, Ambedkar started a new career for himself by starting legal practice at Bombay High Court. He started a Marathi fortnightly, *'Mook Nayak'* (Leader of the Dumb) in 1919. Just like Gandhiji who started *'Young India'* and *'Harijan'*, Dr. Ambedkar chose his Marathi fortnightly for propagating the cause of improving the conditions of the untouchables. In 1927, he started another Marathi fortnightly *'The Bhahiskrit Bharat'* and a weekly, *'Janata'* in 1930.

In 1929, yet another paper *'Samata'* was launched as the organ of the *'Samaj Samata Sangh'*. The itch in him to make his presence felt in the larger community and society at large, made him bold enough to jump into the mainstream to take his fight to logical conclusion. As he himself belonged to the untouchable class, Ambedkar made emancipation of the depressed classes of India his life-mission. His brain-child, *'Samaj Samata Sangh'* was meant for preaching social equality among the untouchables and caste Hindus. Inter-caste marriages and Inter-caste dinners formed important parts of the programme of the organisation.

Not content with mere preaching and writing to secure justice for the untouchables, Ambedkar took to the path of fighting agitation. In December 1927, he led a *satyagraha* to establish the civic rights of the untouchables to draw water from a public tank at Mahad in Kolaba district.

The entry of untouchables in a temple at Nasik was yet another form of agitation he had conceived.

The Communal Award of 1932 conceding separate electorate to the untouchables was opposed by Mahatma Gandhi who went on a fast unto death in protest against it. The Poona Pact provided for reservation of seats for the untouchables in the General constituencies. Ambedkar could not reconcile himself to the political compromise which did not eliminate the social stigma attached to the Harijans (the name given to the untouchables by Gandhiji). As he felt that the Harijans would never get recognition of social equality within the Hindu-fold, he declared that they would leave the Hindu-fold altogether and accept some other religion. He first turned to Sikhism and then to Buddhisms. But this did not alter the real conditions of the Harijans and many of them reverted to their earlier faith.

Whatever opportunity presented itself was seized by Ambedkar to promote the interests of the Harijans. Among his own efforts was the foundation in July, 1945 of the 'People's Education Society' which started a number of Colleges in the then Bombay presidency for Scheduled Caste students.

Though Ambedkar did not look with favour at the Indian National Congress which he regarded as dominated by caste Hindus, during the transfer of power in 1946-47 his eminence as a national leader was fully recognised and he was nominated by the Congress to the Constituent Assembly. He also joined the Nehru Cabinet as the Law Minister. He was the Chairman of the Drafting Committee to frame the Constitution of India and piloted the Bill eminently and successfully, winning encomiums from all quarters.

He was hailed as the *'Modern Manu'* for drafting the Hindu Code Bill in a brilliant manner, and had carved for himself a permanent niche in modern Indian history. His achievements in framing and piloting the Indian Constitution and in preparing the Hindu Code Bill were unique. Even his political adversaries recognised his brilliance and considered him one of the foremost national leaders.

As the Law Minister, Mr. Ambedkar was a revolutionary. He said, "My definition of democracy is a form and method of Government whereby revolutionary changes in the economic and social life of the people are brought about without bloodshed". Then he talked about people; he meant all people who were economically and socially backward. He wanted 'no glaring inequalities' in the society and added "there must not be an oppressed or suppressed class". In other words, he said more emphatically, "There must not be a class which has got all the privileges and a class which has got all the burdens to carry. Such a thing, such a division, such an organisation of society has within itself the germs of bloody revolution, and perhaps it would be impossible for the democracy to cure them".

He resigned as Law Minister in 1951, disappointed over lack of his influence on the government and became a Buddhist. Speaking for the first time in the Constituent Assembly, on December 15, 1946, Dr. Ambedkar declared, "I have no hesitation in saying that, notwithstanding the agitation of the League (Muslim League) for the partition of India, some day enough light will dawn upon the Muslims themselves and they too,will begin to think that a United India is better for everybody".

So, Dr. Ambedkar's views on religion, economics and politics have more relevance today. His birth centenary should be the occasion for all of us to read and comprehend what this stalwart stood for in the totality of Indian polity. He lived up to his own ideal of a 'Great Man'. Greatness was not thrust on him, but he acquired Greatness through his tireless work espousing the cause of his own brethren.

On the Constitution of India, of which he was himself the Chairman of the Drafting Committee, Dr. Ambedkar made it clear "...... Many people seem to be very enthusiastic about the Constitution. Well, I am afraid, I am not. I am quite prepared to join that body of people who want to abolish the Constitution, at any rate to redraft it. But what we forget is that we have a Constitution which contains legal provisions, only a skeleton. The flesh of that skeleton is to be found in what we call constitutional morality. However, in England it is called the Conventions of the Constitution and people must be ready to observe the rules of the game".

That over the recent years, we have not observed the rules of the game is very true. If democracy has to succeed anywhere, we have to learn to observe the rules of the game. This has more relevance to the present day politics, where conventions have been thrown to the winds to make the Constitution a mere piece of paper and not a sacred document.

Besides being one of the founders of our Young Republic (Jan. 26, 1950), its Law Minister and a distinguished academician, Dr. Ambedkar was also a redeemer and an architect of Secular India.

Ambedkar was a multi-faceted personality. He was a prolific writer and was the author of a large number of books. They included: 'Caste in India', 'The Problem of the Rupee', 'Evolution of Provincial Finance in British India', 'Thoughts on Pakistan', 'Ranade, Gandhi and Jinnah', 'Thought on Linguistic States', etc.

Dr. Ambedkar played a crucial role in drawing the attention of the people of India to the pitiable social and economic conditions of a large segment of the Indian population and highlighting the need for providing social and economic justice to them. He succeeded in his lifetime to some extent in bettering the lot of these children of GOD and he will be remembered along with Gandhiji for the humanitarian work, though their methods to attain the goal were different.

Dr. Ambedkar was the first distinguished Indian who was born untouchable and knew what it was to suffer social indignity. On October 3, 1954, Dr. Ambedkar declared in a broadcast talk over All India Radio: "Positively, my social philosophy may be said to be enshrined in three words—liberty, equality and fraternity. My philosophy has roots in religion and not in political science. I have derived them from the teachings of my master, the Buddha".

Following his magnum opus, "The Buddha and His Gospel" completed, he embraced Buddhism on October 14, 1956, at Nagpur along with three lakhs of his followers.

It is a known fact that Buddhists do not believe in a personal God, but believe in Dhamma, which might be called 'good' principle for life management.

Dr. Ambedkar had seen life as it came and came out unscathed through several vicissitudes. But the transformation did come, when he was recognised as a 'man par excellence', after he fought for social justice, for the under-dog, the have-nots and the down-trodden. His was the voice of the Dalits.

Being an intellectual giant, the word 'Buddha' and 'Dhamma' gave him a new light, for, the word 'Buddha-Dhamma' means the nature of an enlightened person, which in other words meant, "All persons, whoever they may be, if they are really and fully enlightened, must have the same nature; that is, total freedom from craving, aversion and delusion".

After having risen to such international heights, Dr. Ambedkar chose to embrace Buddhism. Buddhism was not mere myth but a reality for him. Therefore, those who call themselves as the followers of this great leader must remember that he took to Buddhism after having religiously followed the high ideals that the Buddha had lived and practised in his life, which can be summarised in the words of the Buddha himself :

1. Not to associate with fools; 2. to associate with the wise; 3. to honour those worthy of honour; 4. to live in suitable region; 5. to have accumulated merits of the past; 6. to be rightly concentrated on oneself; 7. to acquire various arts; 8. to master various skills; 9. to be well disciplined; 10. to be well learned; 11. to serve one's parents; 12. to look after one's family; 13. to have pleasant speech; 14. to be peaceful in one's actions; 15. to donate generously; 16. to live the life of Dhamma; 17. to help one's relatives; 18. to abstain from immoral livelihood; 19. to abstain from evil (physical and mental); 20. to abstain from intoxicants; 21. to practice Dhamma diligently; 22. to be respectful; 23. to be humble; 24. to be contented; 25. to be grateful; 26. to listen Dhamma at appropriate time; 27. to be tolerant; 28. to be obedient; 29. to see saintly people; 30. to discuss Dhamma; 31. to meditate; 32. to observe celibacy; 33. to observe noble truths; 34. to realise Nibbana; 35. to remain equanimous while coming in contact with vicissitudes of life; 36. to remain free from sorrow; 37. to remain free from impunity; and 38. to remain free from insecurity.

It should be remembered here that Buddhism is not fundamentally different from Hinduism though it has earned separate status. Interestingly, Buddhism had greatly contributed to Hindu philosophy. The best part of Buddhism was adopted and assimilated by Hinduism. A great writer had said, "Buddhism may differ in certain points from the system of Brahminism and Vedantism but in broad outline, Buddha's system of practical ethics is undoubtedly a child of Vedantism. The fundamental doctrine of truthfulness, charity, philosophy, justice, tolerance and fraternity, are but the echoes of preachings of sublime Vedas".

After embracing Buddhism, Dr. Ambedkar did not live for long. If he had lived a decade more, perhaps he would have brought about a total revolution in man-making education and given the country the much-needed value system based on the highest ideal of Buddha Dhamma. His last words were : *"Buddham Saranam Gachami"*.

And, when he acknowledged the Buddha as his master, he only confirmed that he was a great humanist, reaffirming as it were, what his master had said: "You have been abusing me, but I have not accepted the abuse, so have been left with it". This was his life's highest attainment.

Men born in aristocratic families could easily become great in a capitalist society, with all avenues and opportunities open to them to become great and to be made great. But Bhimrao Ambedkar who rose from the dust could write the lines and chapters of history. He rode like a Colossus on the Indian political scene both in the pre and post-Independence days.

Gandhiji waged a crusade against 'Untouchability' while Ambedkar lead a crusade against "casteism".

Ambedkar was brutally frank when he coined a slogan, "Tell the slave, he is a slave and he will revolt". The slogan has since gained increased currency and relevance today.

And, it is no wonder that positions of honour and prestige came in search of him and he never went about his way in search of honour and prestige which is the order of the day. Do you get me, now?

2

Dr. Ambedkar and Minorities

*Prof. Mumtaz Ali Khan**

Social Reformer

Dr. Baba Saheb Ambedkar was a committed social reformer. His primary concern was to end socio-economic exploitation, discrimination and deprivation. He was very firm in his approach to many serious social evils in practice in the Indian social system. He was a crusader against the practice of untouchability. Caste hierarchical system had dehumanised the lower castes. He therefore did his best to correct the social imbalances to the best of his ability. It is true that he could not see the results of his efforts during his life time. But he had created a strong social movement which is now seen in the country.

Baba Saheb had a deep social vision and penetrative thinking. He had made a deep study of the Indian social system. Indian society is widely known for its religious and caste groups based on well recognized principles. He had seen how these religious and caste considerations had worked to the disadvantage of the religious minorities, linguistic minorities and lower castes.

Social mobility among these groups was very much affected because of the prejudices developed against them by the major Hindu groups. On one hand, Partition of India resulting in the creation of Pakistan had adverse effects on the social relationship between the Muslims and the Hindus. Group prejudices had taken deep roots in the minds of some Hindu social groups.

The post-Partition period had witnessed a devastating effect on the Muslims. Prominent Muslim leaders had migrated to Pakistan, leaving behind a few nationalist Muslims who were respected by the Hindu society. But they too had some initial hurdles and reservation in creating a new social climate to retain

---

* Director, Centre for Research and Development of Dalits, Bangalore-32.

Hindu-Muslim unity and understanding and also promoting confidence among the Muslims in particular.

It was at this crucial social situation where Muslims needed non-Muslims to take up their cause. Though the Muslim League leaders were still dominant, Muslim League's image had been severely damaged. When the making of the Constitution of India was under process, there was a great need to have a great constitutional expert with total commitment to secularism and to the interest of Muslims. There was none other than Dr. B.R. Ambedkar.

Baba Saheb's contribution was not confined to the rehabilitation of the Scheduled Castes only. Often people out of ignorance consider him to be the champion of the Scheduled Castes. But his contribution to other neglected sections is equally significant. His ideas to put an end to the social inequalities, discrimination and denial of opportunities for development among minorities are well founded, but not understood by the minorities themselves. In this paper, an attempt is made to present in brief the monumental contribution made by him to the question of the minorities.

Minority—A Conceptual Clarity

Baba Saheb was not a Sociologist in the technical sense of the term. But there was abundant sociological thinking in him. He was aware of the fact that the Indian society is multi-structured where religious pluralism and cultural dualism prevail. When he had an opportunity to examine the status of the minorities, he did not fail in his duty. 'Minoritism' has acquired a negative meaning today. Some Hindus think that the minorities are pampered and appeased for political ends. But quite after these groups fail to realise that in any democratic set up, minorities do surface and they have their own legitimate place. But none had attempted to give a correct understanding of the term 'Minorities' and their position in free India. It was Dr. Ambedkar who made a dispassionate attempt to analyse the concept of 'Minorities' and justified special safeguards for them.

According to him, the term 'Minorities' is not merely confined to technical sense. This term is not applicable to the religious minorities only. In his opinion, it includes cultural and linguistic minorities also. It is this interpretation of Baba Saheb that has helped today a number of linguistic groups in Karnataka State to get the benefits of certain protected considerations. The linguistic minorities of South Canara, Andhra Pradesh and Tamil Nadu living in Karnataka State have been richly benefited in matters relating to educational institutions. But hardly do these people realise that they are getting the advantages because of the contribution made by Baba Saheb in the Constituent Assembly debates.

In the original provision made by the Sub-committee on Minorities, the intervention of the State to look into the problems of the minorities was only in the nature of a duty cast on the State. It did not amount to a Fundamental Right. This would definitely have made a lot of difference. None realized the implications, not even the members of the Minority groups. It was a crucial issue. Dr. Ambedkar was dissatisfied with this philosophical approach. He said, "... it depended upon the good will of the State. The present situation as you find it ... is that we have converted that into a Fundamental Right so that if a State made any law which was inconsistent with the provisions of this Article, then that law would be invalid."[1] This would therefore ensure uniformity throughout the country and would not be left to the discretion of different political parties ruling in different States.

Social Discrimination

Indian Society is highly fragmented into religious and caste groups. It is a multi-structured society. The peculiar hierarchical system that has been operating in India, over centuries carries with it the axis of pollution and purity on one hand, and dominant Hindu religious groups as against the minority religious groups.

The Hindus by virtue of their 80% population have a natural tendency to control the affairs of the Indian social scene. It is also true that there are internal struggles based on caste considerations. The caste-Hindus try to have a greater share than the lower castes. Thus, social as well as economic inequalities are created, justified and perpetuated.

Then the relationship between the majority Hindu religious groups and the minority religious groups would be subjected to further inequalities. Social discrimination against the minorities is still in practice in some form or the other in our social system. Social discrimination is a well accepted feature of any society where the dominant and the weaker members have to co-exist. It is the tendency on the part of the dominant groups to corner as much as possible all the fruits of development, never bothering about the fact that there are others also waiting for their turn. Baba Saheb was quite alive to this social situation. Therefore, he pleaded that discrimination against a citizen by Government Officers in public administration or by private employers on the ground of race or creed or social status shall be treated as an offence. Such an offence, according to him, should be tried by tribunals for this purpose.

This idea of Baba Saheb is quite revolutionary and practical. When we examine the present style of functioning of the judiciary, we notice that justice is often delayed and ultimately perhaps denied. Tribunals set up for this purpose would give effective and quick remedy or relief to the minorities. Of late, a number of tribunals and forums have been set up. Administrative tribunals at the State level as well as Central levels are doing excellent job in protecting the aggrieved employees. Similarly, a number of consumer forums have been set up to protect the interest of the consumers. Further, a number of land tribunals have been established to protect the interest of the tenants. When there is an imperative need to have such tribunals and they are rendering great service to those whose rights are affected, tribunals to safeguard the interest of the minorities would have helped the minorities whose justifiable rights are often curtailed. But unfortunately, there were not enough members to support Dr. Ambedkar.

He strongly argued that discrimination and fundamental rights are interlinked. He said, "Discrimination was a menace to be guarded against if the Fundamental Rights were to be real." "In a country like India", he said, where it was possible for discrimination to be practised on a vast scale and in a relentless manner, Fundamental Rights could have no meaning unless provision was made for protection against discrimination on the ground of race, creed or social status."[2]

He argued that all citizens shall have equal access to all institutions, conveniences and amenities maintained by or for the public.

Equality of Opportunity

He was conscious of the fact that in a Hindu dominated society or language dominated State, the minorities, religious as well as linguistic, would have to face threats from the majority. He therefore, argued that equality of opportunity should be given to all citizens irrespective of their religion or language. According to him, the minorities should have guaranteed liberty of conscious and free exercise of their religion including right to profess, to preach and to convert within limits compatible with public order and morality. He was broadly in agreement with Munshiji in this regard. But Ambedkar added the words, 'freedom to preach and convert'. He wanted every religious association to be free to regulate and administer its affairs within the limits of the laws applicable to all.

There was a controversy about imparting religious instructions in educational institutions. It is generally believed that there is a tendency on the part of the management of the educational institutions run privately to allow reading of sayings or principles of a particular religion to which the management belongs. In a school or college, there will be children from different religious groups, of course in varying numbers. If the teachings of a religion to which either the majority of the students or staff or management belong are allowed, then it would amount to influencing and conditioning the mind of the young children.

But the religious minorities, particularly the Christians do believe in imparting some teachings of the founders of their religion. Even the very morning prayer would be based on this. Whether this could be allowed? Whether they have the necessary authority to impart religious teachings in the classroom when students of different faiths are present? There were heated discussions over this issue. It is here that Dr. Ambedkar displayed his stewardship, insights and ability. Ambedkar was aware of the mind of the minority educational institutions. His opinion was that religious instructions could be imparted even compulsorily in a school run exclusively for its pupils. But he was equally firm in his views that if such a school receives grants from the State, it shall not make religious instructions compulsory for all the pupils. If done so, if would be unjust.

Right to Educational Institutions

Another significant contribution of Baba Saheb to the development of the minorities relates to the right of the minorities to establish and administer educational institutions. His argument was that every minority group has a right to use its own language. The State shall not enact laws which may go against the interest of the language of the minorities. It is also pointed out where all minorities were free to establish and administer educational institutions of their choice, the State shall not discriminate in extending financial assistance. There was a very serious intervention in this regard from Mahavir Thyagi. Thyagi wanted that the discussion and decision on the rights of the minorities could be delayed for some time to find out what Pakistan would do. This was also the time when Pakistan was drafting its own Constitution. In Pakistan too there were a large number of non-Muslims. Pakistani leaders were harping upon creating an Islamic State. To what extent the Pakistani leaders would guarantee certain special rights to the minorities was definitely a matter of great concern to the Indian political leaders. It could not be one-way traffic. Therefore, Mahavir Thyagi's intervention had good support from some other members of the Drafting Committee and the members of the Constituent Assembly. It looked certain that Thyagi would win his battle.

At this stage Dr. Ambedkar intervened and advanced his thoughtful arguments to counter Thyagi. He did not agree. He said that this approach would be relative. While strongly deprecating this idea of Thyagi, he said that the minorities of India should have absolute rights and should not be related to what Pakistan would do.

Of late, there has been a hue and cry about implementation of Common Civil Code. During the deliberations in the Constituent Assembly. M.R. Masani, Hansa Mehta and Raj Kumari Amrit Kaur wanted Common Civil Code to ensure national interest. At this stage, Baba Saheb was of the firm view that Common Civil Code was eminently desirable, but its application should be entirely on voluntary basis. His contention was fully upheld.

Ambedkar was of the view that the States shall not recognize any religion or have a State religion. He was in favour of religious associations which should be guaranteed freedom of activities within certain reasonable limits.

Agency to Monitor

In order to monitor the implementation of all these rights of the Minorities, he suggested that the Office of Superintendent of Minority Affairs similar to the Auditor General of India be created under section 166 of the Government of India Act. He should be removed in like manner and on the like grounds as a judge of the Supreme Court. At present, there are Minority Commissions set up by the Central Government and some State Governments. But when we attempt a comparative analysis, we find that these are mostly ornamental institutions. Ambedkar would not have allowed such teethless bodies.

Thus, Baba Saheb Ambedkar championed the cause of the minorities of India. His argument was so logical and forceful that ultimatly his suggestions would prevail. That he was a genius, though from an untouchable family, was recognised and appreciated. Had he not championed the case of the minorities what would have been the fate of these people today in the light of struggle for power, position and rights among the major caste groups in the Hindu society? Minorities would not have had their right to establish and administer minority educational institutions. Conversions even in the normal course would have led to serious problems. Common Civil Code would have been forced on the religious Minorities. The country has been witnessing of late public debates and Controversies over implementation of Common Civil Code under Art 44 of the Constitution. In this heated social climate, none including the religious minorities either know or remember the timely intervention of Baba Saheb in offering a conditional support to the demand for implementing the code.

Minorities Ungrateful

It is very unfortunate that Minorities, both religious and linguistic, who enjoy all rights and privileges enshrined in the

Constitution forget that these are the gift of Baba Saheb Ambedkar to them. They have not even publicly or privately paid homage to a man but for whom they would have been in a different social climate. It is also true that by and large they are ignorant of his contribution. It is high time that the intellectuals among the minorities rise to the occasion, understand his contribution and propagate this among the general public.

References

1. Constituent Assembly Debates, Vol. VII, pp. 919-22.
2. Art. 11(11)(3), Select Documents, pp. 98-99.

3

Dr. Ambedkar's Thoughts and Their Relevance in the Present Times

*Dr. T.V. Narayana**

There are three important phases of the life and struggle of Baba Saheb Ambedkar. The first phase relates to the relentless struggle he waged against abolition of untouchability and annihilation of caste system and the battles he fought almost single-handed against the biggest leaders of the country and succeeded in convincing them that there was a very genuine problem of the down-trodden untouchables and the need for doing justice to them in all walks of life. He could convince the then leaders of the greatest political organisation namely the Indian National Congress that there must be reservations to the Scheduled Castes in all branches of administration. This phase constitutes his memorable fight at the Round Table Conferences, his *satyagraha* at Mahad and temple entry at Kaliram. The culmination of this phase is the Poona Pact.

The second phase begins with his maiden memorable speech in the Constituent Assembly which completely turned the tide in his favour. All those who scoffed at him turned to praise him as a great patriot. The countrymen recognised his intellectual ability and realised that he was a great constitutional expert. The Congress leaders entrusted to him the onerous work of drafting the Constitution. He was made the Chairman of the Drafting Committee of the Constitution. He proved his mettle and won admiration of all members of the Assembly. Laurels were showered on him when he completed the work and introduced the Constitution in the Assembly. He could incorporate

* Ex-Member, Andhra Pradesh Public Service Commission, Hyderabad.

guarantees to his people in the Constitution. He worked as the Minister of Law in the first Cabinet of free India of Pandit Jawaharlal Nehru. This phase ends when he resigned from the Cabinet after his failure to get the Hindu Code Bill in full measure to his satisfaction.

The third phase begins when after resigning from the Nehru Cabinet he rejoined the ranks of opposition leaders in the Parliament. He renounces Hinduism, embraces Buddhism, and establishes the Republican Party. He completes his Magnum Opus, the "Buddha and his Dhamma." His health fails. He attains Parinirvana.

In all these three phases of his life what Dr. Baba Saheb has done and said are very much relevant to our times also. His social philosophy will continue to inspire the down-trodden, the depressed and the socially segregated all over the world till social democracy is established in their respective societies. In our own country, relentless fight for social equality for abolition of untouchability and annihilation of casteism will inspire the victims of this scourge till these inhuman practices are put to an end.

Baba Saheb wanted that *Varna Vyavastha* should go away lock, stock and barrel and liberty, equality and fraternity are established in the Hindu society if national integration is to be strengthened and fostered.

Everyday just as we open the newspaper we read headlines stating that atrocities are inflicted upon Scheduled Castes. Innocent people are butchered for no fault of theirs. Their women are raped, their houses are looted and their huts are burnt to ashes. Karmchedu, Neerukonda, Padiri Kuppam and of late Tsundur wherein scheduled castes men were massacred. Their only fault being that they wanted to assert their right of self-respect.

Baba Saheb had shown the way in his own life, as to how these indignities must be fought. The Scheduled Castes must unite and agitate. The *Maha Satyagraha* he launched shows the way. His *satyagraha* for entry into Kaliram temple gives the direction. Non-violent mass resentment and constitutional ways securing justice must be followed. Relentless struggle is the only way.

In the second stage of his life he joined Nehru Cabinet and framed the Constitution. His peroration after he introduced the Constitution, reveals what a great patriot and nationalist he was. He enumerated the ways of maintaining the democracy. He said, "the first thing they must do was to hold fast to the constitutional methods of achieving their social and economic objectives and abandon the methods of civil disobedience, non-cooperation and *satyagraha*, for these methods were nothing but the grammar of anarchy". He advised the political parties not to place their creed above the country.

"He asked his people to shed a narrow outlook and think in terms of the welfare and prosperity of the nation as a whole". He stated that "so far the country's future had not occupied any place in their thought. But now the time had come to think in terms of the wider interest of the nation as a whole". He, therefore, urged his people not to maintain their separate entity and asked them to win sympathies of all the political parties in the country. (Page 419 Dr. Ambedkar and Life admission by Dhananjaya Keer).

Dr. Ambedkar's sayings and sermons will continue to inspire us, enthuse us, direct us for all times to come. He exhorted his people to get educated. Then only their woes will come to an end. At one stage he said, "Education without character is useless". He wanted his people not to be meek as goats and lambs but to be brave like lions. He said they should cultivate Sheel and Shakti. "Self respect and self-reliance are the noble qualities they should endeavour to imbibe". He sermonised that, "the goal of man's life is not reached unless and until he has fully cultivated his mind". Dr. Ambedkar had by his relentless struggle secured constitutional guarantees to us by way of carving reservations in all branches of administration. But when he found the educated among the Scheduled Castes who occupied high positions forgot their own kith and kin who were still poor and suffered from poverty, he was very much pained and called them second class brahmins. He advised them not to behave as such and not to forget their duties towards their unfortunate brethren but to lend them a helping hand.

He visualised that very soon a time will dawn when the present down-trodden people will no more be the ruled but will be the rulers of this great country. In his prophetic words he exhorted his people to train themselves, educate themselves, prepare themselves and to equip themselves to become fit enough to man as leaders in all walks of life and in all branches of administration. He exhorted the young educated men of his community to prove themselves to be second to none in whatever work is entrusted to them.

Baba Saheb's speeches and exhortations are like sermons and are sure to guide and direct not only his people but all the people of the country. In one of his speeches before Independence speaking of his people he stated, "the surest way for the salvation lies in higher education, higher employment and better ways of earning a living". On another occasion, he said, "self-elevation is not achieved by the blessings of others but only by ones' own struggle and deed". As long ago as 1927, in his speech during *Maha Satyagraha* he said, "we will attain self-elevation only if we learn self-help, regain our self-respect and gain self-knowledge". He advised his people to learn to be clean. "Keep away from vices, give education to your children. Instil ambition into them, inculcate in their minds that they are destined to be great".

He said, "Do not believe in fate but have faith in hard work. Sacrifice the present pleasures for a great future". He called upon his countrymen to shed casteism. He said in this country caste has made public opinion impossible. "Virtue has become caste-ridden and morality has become caste-bound. The real remedy for breaking caste is inter-marriage. Nothing else will serve as the solvent of caste." In pre-Independence days speaking about religious conversion about the Scheduled Castes he categorically stated that "they should not at any cost be denationalized. Their numerical strength should not be dwindled." As a noble, wise and true son of India he advised the Scheduled Castes that they should help in the destiny of the country and in the political advancement of the country.

The advice Baba Saheb gave to social workers and public servants is so exalting and very much relevant not only now but for all times to come. He sermonised, "blessed are those who are awakened to their duty to those among whom they are born. Glory to those who devote their time and talents and their all to the annihilation of slavery".

If only the leaders, officers and the educated among the Scheduled Castes follow the above advice sincerely in the true spirit and act accordingly their development and the progress will be hastened up four-fold.

In the evening of his life Baba Saheb embraced Buddhism. The reason for his conversion to Buddhism was that there was social democracy, equality, liberty and fraternity in that religion. By conversion the Scheduled Castes would still be in the main national stream of the country.

Buddhism is a way of life which teaches people to inculcate in themselves, *Maitri*, *Karuna* and *Pragna*. The Dhamma of Buddha teaches: (1) the path of purity, (2) the path of righteousness, and (3) the path of virtue. If the Scheduled Castes could practice these essentials of Dhamma they could well be ideal and noble men free from all sufferings.

The exhortation that Baba Saheb gave us was, "Lost rights are never regained by begging and by appeals to the conscience of the usurpers but by relentless struggle". Scheduled Caste people will attain their goal of equality with others by only following Baba Saheb's message.

Baba Saheb was a national leader and a great patriot who said,"we must be determined to defend our independence till the last drop of our blood".

The clarion call he gave to the Nation in the Constituent Assembly after introducing the Constitution is valid even now, on Jan. 26, 1950. "We have equality in politics and inequality in social and economic life. We must remove this contradiction at the earliest moment or else those who suffer from inequality will blow up the structure of political democracy". If only our national leaders pay heed to this warning there will be social justice and economic equality in our society.

4

Dr. Ambedkar and Education

*J.V. Raghavendra Rao**

Dr. Ambedkar was one of those "wretched of the earth"[1], "the lowliest and the lost"[2] of the Indian soil who, by sheer articulation of this genius and prodigious industry, shot into the political horizon as a spectacular leader and an outstanding intellectual. He is to be reckoned with not only as a political emancipator, economic historian and extraordinary jurist and constitutionalist but a great savant and educationist too. Secondly, the spectrum of his ideas or action has not only influenced the process of emancipation of Scheduled Castes but many others too. In this paper, an endeavour is made to assess Ambedkar's ideas in respect of education and also how education has influenced his outlook and action. The intent is to probe deep and critically evaluate the content and meaning of his ideas. This, inter alia, cannot be undertaken in separation from the biographical and the social context of his life.

Dr. Ambedkar was born in 1891 in a Mahar family, of Central India, whose social rank was very low. His father, a subedar major, was overly burdened with 14 children and Ambedkar happened to be the last one. His father, obviously, had not enough financial means to support Ambedkar's studies. Ambedkar reached his high school studies in Parel, Bombay. He used to take his afternoon meals in the school and had no home support to buy books of his interest and choice. An avid and keen reader that Ambedkar was he had to help himself with reading in public libraries. This left a deep impression on his love for education and its difussion among the dalits too. This later caused the formation of People's Education Society in Bombay. The impact of his mentor Jotiba Phuley is also revealed

---

* Professor, Department of Sociology, Osmania University, Hyderabad-500007.

in the inauguration of Siddhartha College, 20 June, 1946. Here, we also like to make an interesting observation regarding the naming of the college, when a lone Mahar boy like Ambedkar passed his Matriculation examination in 1907, the event became a matter of pride and celebration for the family and friends. On this occasion one of his teachers K.A. Keluskar presented him with a copy of the Buddha's life.[3] His appreciation of rational and skeptic personality and leadership of Buddha which had a great impact on his religious as well as secular thinking, pushed him into the charismatic fold of Buddhism. Naming the College, hence, appears to be a personal tribute of Ambedkar to Buddha whose inspiration has directed his thinking and activities in many secular matters including education.

Ambedkar happens to be one of the few Mahar pupils who could go abroad for higher studies. With the help of a scholarship from Maharaja Sayajirao Gaekwad of Baroda, he went to the University of Columbia in America, from where he obtained his Masters as well as Ph.D. Degrees. Among the professors who influenced him, a notable individuality was[4] John Dewey. John Dewey was a philosopher of rationalism and pragmatism. He also wrote prolifically on American educational system and culture. He had a great belief in the uses of education and its potentialities to alter the values of individuals and prepare them for change. Greatly moved by Dewey's ideas on education and also experiencing the values of individual freedom and dignity in American Universities and society, Ambedkar developed almost a doctrinal belief in the efficacious and transformatory character of education. As[5] Dhananjay Keer has observed, Ambedkar believed that increments in education would enhance the abjuration of traditional values and would also inculcate value preparation for change. Education coupled with law would usher in a great degree of social change, for law was the essence of the State.

Another major source of impact on his thinking was[6] M.G. Ranade who was a great advocate of rationalism, evolutionism and modernatism, particularly in politics. Ranade believed that education was the best and surest warranty of social change, for changes primarily have to germinate in the minds of men before they could fruition to its inexorable end. Ambedkar carried in him these ideas and spurned the idea of force as against education as an instrument of social change.

One more aspect of his life profile which glued him to education was his Mahar background. As a student he was not permitted to learn Sanskrit of which he was fond. In the school at Satara where he had his early education he experienced discrimination at the hands of fellow pupils. When his teacher asked Ambedkar to solve a problem in Mathematics which other pupils had failed to solve, he attempted to go to the blackboard to solve the problem. But the fellow students shouted against Ambedkar, for behind the blackboard lay the tiffin boxes of fellow pupils and his writing on the blackboard would lend a defiling touch to the food. Instead of discouraging him this strengthened, fostered the iron will of Ambedkar for learning and education. Additionally, it appears to us that he found a great compensation and rejuvenation for his murky life experiences in the garden of books and public libraries which was strewn with lofty ideas and fruitful lives. Apart from his exciting studies in various libraries in Columbia and New York, his deep apprenticeship at the feet of master whose life-blood was found in the London Museum and India Office Libraries, etc., paved the way for the emergence of Ambedkar as a formidable scholar and a commendable educationist.

Yet another aspect which had a great bearing on his involvement with education was his career development and professional experiences. His post-matric employment in the estate of Maharaja Sayajirao and later employment after his return from his foreign studies in 1917 as a military secretary to the Maharaja, had deeply injured his being, for nobody treated him as a human worthy of dignity and social amity. He was treated by the staff and peons as a despicable object. Similar was the experience in respect of his accommodation and food at the hands of other citizens. This happened to Ambedkar although he was an erudite scholar and a man of enviable academic accomplishments. None of the degrees could alter his status, for he carried the social stigma of a Mahar with him. On November, 1918 he accepted the job as a Professor of Political Economy in Sydenaham College, Bombay until he left for London. Although he worked as a lawyer after his return from London, he had to complement his income by working as a Professor of Mercantile

Law on a part-time basis for three years at Batliboy Accountancy Institute. He also worked as an examiner for the Bombay University. After four years Ambedkar became a full Professor in Government Law College, Bombay. His interaction with students and teachers have influenced his ideas on education although some experiences have been dark and disappointing. Subsequently, his assumption of the post of Principal of the Government Law College of Bombay in June, 1935 enabled him to get insights into academic and administrative problems. His three years experience as the Principal and also Membership of Legislative Council of the Province of Bombay provided rich experience of the need as well as the complexity of problems of education, particularly, with regard to the exploited people of Mahar community.

The other important dimension which can explain partly his commitment to educational values as a means as well as an end lies in the *Weltanschuang* (World-view) of the times shared by many leaders from Dada Bhai Naroji to Tilak, Phule, Ranade and Gokhale etc. Almost from the times of Rammohan Roy, the innovative leaders of India have been championing the course of English education for it was a source of new knowledge, national thinking and humanistic way of life. Unexceptionably Ambedkar, too, shared the concern for education in general and the education of the Mahars in particular. The Mahars were steeped in illiteracy and superstitions like the "Karma" doctrine etc., living the life of dehumanised and brutalised beings. Ambedkar firmly believed that education could bring not only a new consciousness among Mahars but also impell them towards praxis of self-liberation.

Ambedkar sought his inspiration for practical politics from Jyotiba Phule and Justice Ranade. Apart from running journals, writing petitions and drafting manifestos he also sought to realise the idea of Dalit Liberation by starting many schools. In fact, he had an early encounter with V.R. Shinde in 1920 at Nagpur, regarding the self-management and initiative of educational institutions by SCs themselves. He started the Siddhartha College in 1945 at Bombay under the auspices of People's Education Society. Later, Colleges of Law and Commerce were added. In Aurangabad, the Milind College, the Ambedkar College in Mahad and another Ambedkar College run by neo-Buddhists at

Nagpur etc., are the signal achievements of Ambedkar and his followers. These institutions, later, have been followed by a complex of institutions started for the enlightenment and upliftment of the depressed classes.

Hitherto, we have presented the biographical and social context of Ambedkar relative to his ideas on education. Now the discussion proper is in order.

Ambedkar's basic educational philosophy is seen in the two objectives which govern the inauguration of Peoples Education Society, Bombay. They are (a) the search for truth and (b) to practise humanitarian principles in one's life. The Buddhist principles of *Prajna* (Understanding) and *Karuna* (Compassion) seems to have been the beacon lights of not only a major part of his life but also his perspective of education. Inspired as he was by the rational approach of the Buddha in the east and John Dewey in the west he called for inculcation of rational thinking and scientific temper among masses in general and students, in particular. In his address to Elphinston College, Bombay, in December, 1952 he exhorted the teachers and the taught in the University to meet the requirements as well as challenges of the modern world by production as well as application of knowledge. He warned that Universities should continue to be sacred abodes of learning and not workshop centres which trained an army of clerks. He also hearkened the audience, that the great ideas set by the progenitors of Indian culture, like Ranade and Tilak etc., should be emulated and practised.

For the upliftment of the depressed classes he developed a programme of education as a part of the general manifesto of Indian Labour Party before the general elections of 1937. To stamp out illiteracy, he emphasised the necessity of full and compulsory education, liberal education, he knew was neither useful for the upper classes in the long run nor the depressed classes of the Indian society. He advocated the adoption of diversified technical education. Since many pupils from depressed classes did not have the financial wherewithal to prosecute their studies, he stressed the necessity of scholarships in educational institutions. Another interesting aspect of his programme of education was the divorce he sought between universities and non-teaching universities.

Ambedkar was a great champion of universal primary education. An amendment to the Educational Act in Bombay Legislative Assembly was brought forth by the Education Minister who sought to introduce Charka in the Primary Schools. The Charka scheme drew its inspiration from Gandhi on the principle of 'earning while learning'. Ambedkar contented that the Gandhian Scheme would deprive Scheduled Caste people of the curiosity and adventure of learning for they were the poorest of the social strata. They could be tempted to earn a little more than learn, unless and until education was sought to be made compulsory.

Although Ambedkar started educational institutions through voluntary effort and organisations, he strongly believed in the educational modernization of masses under the auspices of the State. In his concept of State Socialism he allocated a major role for the State in discharging its duties in respect of education of the unlettered millions of citizens in the country.

In respect of teaching in the colleges and universities, Ambedkar was unhappy with colonial system of education, in British and post-Independent India. Inspired by the freedom of choice of learning in American Universities, he advocated a reorganization of subjects and courses to provide a wider exposure of knowledge to the pupils. Based on his first-hand experience he called for removal of inequalities of pay scales and status among academics involved either in teaching or research. He also abhorred the idea of differentiated status for under-graduate and post-graduate colleges within the complex of University system.

Ambedkar was a great lover of students. As a Principal of Government Law College he took keen interest in enriching and expanding library and also in their curricular and extra-curricular requirements and facilities. He was a conscentious teacher and worked hard to deliver his lectures with insight and information. According to him, a Professor "should not only be learned; he must speak in a clear tone. He must be well versed". He also opined that Professors should constantly seek knowledge and try for truth and practise it.

Ambedkar's opinion on education by sex is interesting. He thought liberal education for girls was of no consequence. "What is the use of Burke and Shakespeare to girls"? he said.

Ambedkar wanted women to be more particularly trained in Home Science Education and peripherally in other subjects. Men, of course, are free to pursue a variety of courses and studies.

Ambedkar's life has been a continuum of study and struggle. His academic interest in crucial political and economic problems continued until the end. However, he stated that students in schools and colleges should not be involved in active politics. On the contrary, they should be engaged in the development of self-culture and self-help. Ambedkar exhorted the students to put a premium on industry and creativity. They should persevere to attain goals and ideals dearer to them, devoid of which life becomes less thrilling and meaningful.

Ambedkar's belief about commitment to education is so deep and wide that it has affected the entire gamut of his outlook and activity. In his struggle against the Congress, the Muslim League and the British for the freedom and emancipation of Scheduled Castes he used Parliamentary methods of struggle. He believed in petition, representation and debate as a means of information as well as redressal of social problems. He appeared before many commissions like the Royal Commission on Indian Currency, the Simon Commission and the Round Table Conference, etc., and vigorously pleaded for the upliftment of depressed classes.

In contrast to him, Gandhiji used *satyagraha* and non-cooperation methods as major instruments of struggle. Ambedkar used *satyagraha* only three times in his life when major issues like temple entry in Nasik and land distribution in Vidarbha were at stake. He neither believed in *satyagraha* nor 'change of heart' theory. He wanted to use *satyagraha* even where he launched to educate the masses and ultimately legitimise the gains through the organ of laws. In this respect, Ambedkar's political bias seems to be in favour of Constitutional, Parliamentary and Legalistic methods. Education, after all, is a critical, component of stability and change in the evolutionary process of societies. Since Ambedkar did not embrace the philosophical anarchist in Gandhi nor the proletarian revolutionary in Marx, he emerges as a champion of education and educative struggles for creation of consciousness and liberation of the Dalit masses. Truth for Ambedkar has never been absolute and all his life he was in search of truth which would liberate the Dalits from the oppression of Hinduism. Although it started in 1938 at Nasik, Ambedkar went through a long ordeal of judgment and evaluation before he finally converted largely Mahars into Buddhism. In October, 1956, at Nagpur, his process of learning and unlearning was such that the goals of rationality, brotherhood, and equality of Buddhism had to be adopted. While opinions would differ on the last act of Ambedkar's life namely, conversion to Buddhism, none can doubt his quest for truth as he understood it. "To strive, to seek, to find and not to yield" was the summum bonum of his life and it's a source of education for all who participate in that adventure.

References

1. Frantz Fannon's famous revolutionary expression, which is also the title of his thesis.
2. Rabindranath Tagore's Poetic Phrase for the deprived and oppressed strata in "Geetanjali".
   "Here is thy foot stool, here rest thy feet.
   Where live the lowliest and the lost".
3. M. Sriram Murthy and P. Satyanarayana-*Ambedkar - the Awakener of Dalit Masses* (Telugu), p.18.
4. G.S. Lokhande, *Bhimrao Romji Ambedkar*, Sterling Publishers, New Delhi, 1977, p.10.
5. Dhananjay Keer, *Ambedkar : Life and Mission* (Popular Prakashan, Bombay), 1961, p. 441.
6. W.N. Kuber, *Ambedkar : A Critical Study*, People's Publishing House, New Delhi, 1973, p.20.

5

Emancipation of SCs/STs : Facts and Fallacies

*Dr. B. Gopal**

Of the various daunting tasks confronting the Constitution makers, the most important one was the one relating to the all-round upliftment of those belonging to the Scheduled Castes and Scheduled Tribes who constitute a little over 22% of the country's population.[1] The hopes and aspirations of these people found expression through the personality of their greatest leader until now, Dr. B.R. Ambedkar who launched a life-long crusade for their emancipation from centuries old enslavement and ostracism.[2] They were leading a life of rank poverty, illiteracy and utter backwardness,[3] and socially were not even part of the system and were treated with contempt and lack of human consideration.[4] In order therefore to improve the socio-economic conditions of these sections in society, Dr. Ambedkar had played the part of destiny. For this purpose, he was committed to the road of peaceful transformation and was against any means which involved resort to violence and turmoil.[5]

Dr. Ambedkar contemplated various means for raising the socio-economic status of SCs and STs[6]. However, it was primarily through the numerous safeguards incorporated into the Indian Constitution, of which he himself was the chief architect, that he hoped to arm them with political power, to improve their socio-economic, educational and cultural conditions, and to actualise their gradual deliverance from rhetoric to reality, from deprivation to development, from social stigma and suffering to social respect, solace, and equality.[7]

---

* Professor, Department of Political Science, Osmania University, Hyderabad.

The specific constitutional provisions intended to safeguard the interests of the SCs and STs are[8]—

(1) Art.17 : Abolition of untouchability and prohibition of its practice in any form;

(2) Art. 23 : Prohibition of *'begar'*, or forced or bonded labour;

(3) Art. 335 : Reservations for SCs and STs in appointments to services and posts in connection with the affairs of the Union of State; and

(4) Reservation of seats in proportion to their numbers for the SCs and STs in the Lok Sabha (Art. 330) and in the Vidhan Sabhas (Art. 332).

Some of the other provisions also sought to reinforce the status of the SCs and STs as a 'protected weaker section'. They include the anti-discriminatory and formal equality provisions of the Constitution, empowering the State to make any provision for the advancement of any socially and educationally backward class of citizens : Art.15(4), and for the reservation of appointments or posts in favour of any backward class of citizens which in the opinion of the State is not adequately represented : Art.16(4). Also included is the directive in Article 46 that the State shall promote with special care the educational and economic interests of the weaker sections of the people, and in particular, of SCs and STs, and that it shall protect them from social injustice and all forms of exploitation.[9]

It is over 40 years now since the above provisions have been in practice. This is a long enough period to review the working of those provisions in order to find out as to how much benefit had accrued to the SCs and STs for their all- round development. There could be no better occasion than the centenary of Dr. Ambedkar to take stock of the whole situation and to make a comprehensive assessment regarding the ideal of socio-economic transformation of the depressed sections and what is the real position today. An attempt is, therefore, made in this paper to arrive at the truth.

For an analytical purpose the measures undertaken in pursuance of the various constitutional provisions for the SCs/STs may be treated under three broad categories, viz., protective, developmental, and preferential. Abolition of untouchability and the disabilities arising out of its practice in any form, and prohibition of bonded labour come under the first category. Various educational schemes such as post-matric scholarships and hostels under the Central Sector, and pre-matric stipends, reimbursement of tuition fee, book banks, and hostels under the state sector, special component plans of the Centre, and States special central assistance, and the SCs Development Corporation fall under the second category. Measures like legislative, educational and employment reservations belong to the third category. Of these, the effective implementation of the measures of the first two categories is a pre-condition for actualising the measures of the third category.[10]

Untouchability

One of the scourges of the Indian social system is its caste hierarchy. The SCs are considered to be 'polluting' and their mere touch or shadow is regarded as defiling.[11] They have also been for centuries victims of untouchability.[12]

The Untouchability (Offences) Act of 1955 was intended to wipe out untouchability and the social disabilities arising out of it, by making its practice in any form punishable under law. But, as this Act proved to be too weak and inadequate to meet the constitutional requirement,[13] in November 1976 it was amended and amplified as the Protection of Civil Rights (PCR) Act, 1955, with the resolve to totally eradicate untouchability within five years of its implementation.[14] But, unfortunately even this Act has not fared any better.

Data on PCR cases indicate the persistence of untouchability in virtually all the States. The only State reported to be relatively free from untouchability (and from related atrocities) against the SCs is West Bengal.[15]

Of the yearly average of PCR cases from 1977 to 1985, only about 62 per cent of those registered with the police were 'challaned' or filed before the courts; only about 31 per cent of those before the courts were disposed of; and only about 20 per cent of those disposals ended up in conviction. Stated differently, of the total cases registered with the police on an average not even 10 per cent (including cases brought forward) ended up in conviction.[16]

TABLE -1

Cases involving violation of Protection of Civil Rights Act 1955 against SCs (5 States recording the highest incidence)

Sl. No.	State	1977	1978	1979	1980	1981	1982	1983	1984	1985	Yearly Average
1.	Tamil Nadu	792	547	1157	858	1136	1105	1205	1402	1280	1054
2.	Maharashtra	266	1283	1604	1576	998	769	558	510	NA	840
3.	Karnataka	329	426	550	488	581	674	567	532	659	534
4.	Gujarat	570	716	506	408	281	347	386	271	169	406
5.	Madhya Pradesh	321	398	307	247	237	337	390	370	NA	290

Note : NA— Not Available.

Source : Reports of the Commissioner and the Commission for SCs and STs 1978-79 to 1985-86.

TABLE - 2

PCR Cases by Nature of Disposal — All India

	Police Challaned			*Courts*						
					Disposals					
Year	*Total Cases for disposal*	*In No.*	*As % to total*	*Total Cases for disposal*	*Convicted*	*Acquitted*	*Total*	*Col. 8 as % of Col. 5*	*Col. 6 as % of Col. 8*	*Col. 6 as % of Col.2*
1	2	3	4	5	6	7	8	9	10	11
1977	2799	1325	47.3	5193	551	1463	2014	38.8	27.4	19.7
1978	4976	3751	75.4	7704	490	2002	2492	32.3	19.7	9.8
1979	4769	2662	55.8	5827	261	1069	1330	22.8	19.6	5.5
1980	5230	3550	67.9	9129	1267	2866	4133	45.3	30.7	24.2
1981	4783	2865	59.9	7860	441	2085	2526	32.1	17.5	9.2
1982	4777	2665	55.8	7212	199	1633	1832	25.4	10.9	4.2
1983	4829	2902	60.1	9249	243	1707	1950	21.1	12.5	5.0
1984	4261	2708	63.6	8414	325	1781	2106	25.0	15.4	7.6
1985	2789	1926	69.1	3892	97	1294	1391	35.7	7.0	3.5
Yearly Average	4357	2706	62.1	7164	430	1767	2197	30.7	19.6	9.9

Source : Reports of the Commissioner and the Commission for SCs and STs 1978-79 to 1985-86.

If this all-India pattern is any indication of the poor performance of the PCR Act, data available for some of the States indicate that the variations at the State level have been mostly for the worse despite a relatively higher percentage of 'Challaning' by the police in at least two States (Gujarat and Kranataka), and despite a relatively higher percentage of disposals by the courts in at least one of them (Gujarat) and two other (Keralas and Tamil Nadu), in all the States most of the cases have ended up in acquittals.[17] Stated differently, only less than 9 percent of the cases before the courts and only less than 4 percent of the cases registered with the police have ended up in conviction.[18]

TABLE - 3
PCR Cases by Nature of Disposal : States

Sl. No.	*State*	*Total cases for disposal*	Police			Courts					
			Challaned		*Total Cases for disposal*	*Disposals*					
			In No.	*As % to total*		*Convicted*	*Acquitted*	*Total*	*Col.9 as % of Col.6*	*Col.7 as % of Col.9*	*Col.7 as % of Col.3*
1	2	3	4	5	6	7	8	9	10	11	12
1.	Gujarat	179	153	85.5	484	2	200	202	41.7	1.0	1.1
2.	Karnataka	765	591	77.3	568	2	21	23	4.0	8.7	0.3
3.	Kerala	44	24	54.5	81	0	31	31	38.3	0.0	0.0
4.	Orissa	121	66	54.5	405	2	34	36	8.9	5.6	1.7
5.	Rajasthan	216	108	50.0	446	38	17	55	12.3	69.1	17.6
6.	Tamil Nadu	1393	944	67.8	1853	50	982	1032	55.7	4.8	3.6
	Total	2718	1886	69.4	3837	94	1285	1379	35.9	6.8	3.5

Source : Tabulated from the Commission for SCs and STs, 8th report 1985-86.

While the large number of cases pending with the courts is a reflection of the tardy judicial process, the large number of cases ending up in acquittals is for other reasons as well.[19] As the reports of the Commissioner for SCs and STs indicate, these include the weak socio-economic condition of the victims and their witnesses, land disputes, alienation of tribal land, bonded labour, wage disputes, defective investigation by the police, ineffective or indifferent handling of cases by the prosecution staff, victims yielding to pressures, promises, allurements or intimidation, and the long drawn out trials which alone can discourage any victim from pursuing the case effectively.

TABLE - 4
Atrocity Cases against SCs
(5 States recording highest incidence)

Sl. No.	*States*	*1977*	*1978*	*1979*	*1980*	*1981*	*1982*	*1983*	*1984*	*1985*	*Average*
1.	Madhya Pradesh	3366	3240	3866	3877	4033	4749	5292	6128	4890	4382
2.	Uttar Pradesh	4874	5660	4102	4279	3865	3977	3851	4200	4135	4338
3.	Bihar	681	1911	2153	1890	1983	2073	1809	1845	1402	1750
4.	Rajasthan	261	8886	760	1180	1562	1731	1604	1648	1437	1230
5.	Maharashtran	570	1053	503	518	695	680	704	579	428	637

Source : Reports of the Commissioner and Commission for SCs and STs 1978-79 to 1985-86.

Though the tables give some idea of the persistence of untouchability, they are too inadequate to bring out the real magnitude of this evil. For more often than not most of the cases go unnoticed and unreported. The Seventh Report (1984-85) of the Commissioner for SCs/STs noted that quite a large number of the victims do not seek legal redress and therefore, remain buried in their mental recesses.[20] In this context it would be very pertinent to recall what Gunnar Myrdall stated. Commenting on the subject in a thought-provoking study, he writes : "Thus, the combination of radicalism in principle and conservatism in practice ...... was quickly woven into the fabric of Indian politics. Social legislation pointed the direction in which society should travel, but left the pace indeterminate. Many of these laws were intentionally permissive. In banning .... untouchability, the government did not vigorously seek to enforce its legislation. Laws were either not enforced at all or were not enforced according to their spirit and intention."[21]

Closely related to the persistence of untouchability is the perpetration of atrocities against the SCs. Of late there has been a considerable increase in the number of atrocity cases in several States.[22] Whenever such cases occur, there is an unfortunate tendency to politicise them with the narrow intention of vote-catching.[23]

Of the different types of atrocity cases registered in the whole country, at least one-fourth have involved grievous hurt, followed by arson, rape and murder.[24]

TABLE -5
Atrocity Cases against SCs and type of atrocity
(All India)

Year	*Murder*		*Grievous hurt*		*Rape*		*Arson*		*Others*		*Total*	
	No.	*%*	*No.*	*%*	*No.*	*%*	*No.*	*%*	*No.*	*%*	*No.*	*%*
1977	334	3.1	1341	12.3	332	3.1	716	6.6	8156	75.0	10879	100
1978	457	3.0	1582	10.5	541	3.6	1203	8.0	11287	74.9	15070	100
1979	388	2.8	1441	10.3	430	3.1	1013	7.2	10703	76.6	13975	100
1980	500	3.6	1411	10.2	551	4.0	991	7.1	10413	75.1	13866	100
1981	493	3.4	1492	10.4	604	4.2	1245	8.7	10474	73.2	14308	100
1982	513	3.4	1429	9.5	635	4.2	1035	6.9	11441	76.0	15054	100
1983	525	3.5	1362	9.2	641	4.3	994	6.7	11324	76.3	14846	100
1984	551	3.3	1468	8.9	696	4.2	988	6.0	12883	77.7	16586	100
1985	489	3.3	1357	9.0	674	4.5	972	6.5	11525	76.7	15017	100
Yearly Average	472	3.3	1431	9.9	567	3.9	1017	7.1	10912	75.8	14400	100

Source : Reports of the Commissioner and the Commission for SCs and STs 1978-79 to 1985-86.

The nature of disposal of these cases has not been any better: of the total cases for disposal by the police, not even 100 per cent (including cases brought forward) ended up in conviction.[25] (Table 6)

These cases again do not reflect the real magnitude of atrocities; more so when contrasted against the recurrent press reports from different parts of the country about the crimes on the SCs. According to the report of the National Commission for SCs and STs published in April 1990, 4022 SCs/STs were murdered and crimes against dalits were reported between 1981 and 1986. Given that many crimes go unreported, the number of offences may well be much higher.[26] The reasons mentioned earlier for the PC cases also apply to this and to the large number of cases pending with the courts and ending up in acquittal.[27] The police inaction and complexity were also cited as causes for atrocities on several occasions.[28]

TABLE - 6
Atrocity Cases against SCs and Nature of Disposal

Sl. No.	States	Police			Courts						
		Challaned			Disposals						
		Total cases for disposal	No.	As % to total	Total Cases for disposal	Convicted	Acquitted	Total	Col. 9 as % of Col. 6	Col. 7 as % of Col. 9	Col. 7 as % of Col. 3
1.	Himachal Pradesh	67	48	71.6	174	27	51	78	15.5	34.6	40.3
2.	Karnataka	464	337	72.6	337	3	77	80	0.9	3.8	0.6
3.	Madhya Pradesh	6791	2526	37.2	6472	227	104.	381	4.3	72.7	4.1
4.	Maharashtra	482	356	73.9	1436	176	364	540	12.3	32.6	36.5
5.	Orissa	215	131	60.9	505	4	54	58	0.8	6.9	1.9
6.	Punjab	33	26	78.8	40	2	8	10	5.0	20.0	6.1
7.	Rajasthan	1511	1026	67.9	5905	162	244	406	2.7	39.9	10.7
8.	Tamil Nadu	948	655	69.1	1079	47	419	466	4.4	10.1	5.0
9.	Uttar Pradesh	4826	3017	62.5	15080	803	1536	2339	5.3	34.3	16.6
	Total	15337	8122	53.0	31028	1501	2857	4358	4.8	34.4	9.8

Source : Eighth Report of the Commission for SCs and STs, 1985-86.

The perpetration of atrocities against the SCs is to be partly explained by the increasing resentment of the SCs against the social indignities such as denial of entry into public places of worship, discrimination and differential treatment in hotels and tea stall, refusal of service by washermen and barbers, and restriction on movement in certain localities, on wearing sandals, riding horses, and leading marriage processions through certain caste-Hindu localities.[29] The other major factors listed in the various reports of the Commissioner for SCs and STs include envy of the caste-Hindus for the various welfare measures adopted by the government to ameliorate the socio-economic conditions of the SCs[30], and the increase in awareness on the part of the SCs/STs about their rights, desire to assert them and consequent resistance put up by them against denial of those rights.[31]

Bonded Labour

This practice is rampant in many States.[32] The Bonded Labour System (Abolition) Act of 1976 is intended to abolish this evil practice, and identify, free, and rehabilitate its victims of whom at least 80 percent are reported to be SCs and STs. But its implementation has not served this purpose so far. If the estimate of bonded labourers in the country at about 22.4 lakh (as made by a survey conducted in 1978 by the Gandhi Peace Foundation in collaboration with the National Labour Institute) is any indication, by its implementation the act has so far only scratched the surface.

TABLE - 7
Bonded Labourers Identified, Released and Rehabilitated (1986) (5 States with highest incidence)

Sl. No.	States	Identified and Freed	Rehabilitated	Percentage
1.	Karnataka	62689	40033	63.9
2.	Orissa	42421	30256	71.3
3.	Tamil Nadu	33132	32517	98.1
4.	Andhra Pradesh	24788	18418	74.3
5.	Uttar Pradesh	18334	17662	96.3

Source : Eighth Report of the Commission for SCs & STs.

Economic Dependence

By far the most important cause for the continuing suppression of the SCs/STs is their virtual dependence on the landed gentry for the day-to-day sustenance. Due to this weakness, they are compelled to put up with all sorts of indignities.[33] In 1982, the SCs owned only about 8 percent of the total land in the rural areas of the country as a whole, though their households accounted for about 20 percent of the total rural households.

TABLE - 8
Percentage of SC HHs to Total HHs and Percent of Area Owned by them to Total Area Owned, 1982

Sl. No.	*States*	*Households*	*Area Owned*	*Index of access to Ownership*
1.	West Bengal	29.5	20.6	0.70
2.	Himachal Pradesh	28.0	13.9	0.49
3.	Rajasthan	20.1	12.5	0.62
4.	Uttar Pradesh	24.7	10.5	0.42
5.	Orissa	18.6	9.6	0.52
6.	All India	19.7	7.6	0.40

Source : NSS, 37th round, No. 330, January-December 1982.

This low access to land, the principal resource and the main source of power, dominance, oppression and exploitation in rural India,[34] has several implications. Efforts made at land reforms so that surplus land could be distributed among landless SCs/STs have failed to fructify. For instance, in Andhra Pradesh it was expected that as a result of the Land Reform (Ceiling of Agriculture Holdings) Act, 1973, a minimum of 20 lakh acres of surplus land would be acquired by the government but due to tardy[35] and half-hearted implementation,[36] only 2.46 lakh acres could be acquired.[37] Even the small pieces of land distributed remained on paper. Thus, the vested interests colluded with the bureaucracy to defeat the intention of law-makers and the SCs/STs continue to be denied the land, which alone would bring a marked change in their status. The implications flowing out of low access to land are—

First, the higher percentage of landless households among the SCs compared to the rest of the population. This condition inhibits them from asserting themselves to play a meaningful role in various fields of activity. Wherever this dependence is reduced, as in the case of Mahars in Maharashtra, the SCs have come into their own.[38]

Second, the smaller areas of land owned by most of the SC land owning households. In most States the SC households are conspicuous by their absence or negligible presence in the large ownership category, and by their concentration in the marginal ownership category. That the area of land owned by the SC households in the marginal category is too inadequate for their economic use should be only too obvious from the average size of their holdings in all the ownership categories combined. At the all-India level it is only about one-third of that among the non-SCs. At the State level it is even less.

Third, the greater incidence of poverty among the SCs, and their greater deprivation by and dependence on the caste-Hindus as the Planning Commission's Working Group on SCs and STs (1980-85) reported, the SCs have few assets, "are generally unable to avail themselves of the new employment opportunities generated through various economic development programmes", and "are in fact caught up in a vicious circle in which they are dependent upon their exploiters for their sustenance and are largely denied opportunities to develop the capabilities of attaining an independent livelihood".

Fourth, in the absence of access to land, as either owners or protected tenants, the SCs are forced to eke out a living mostly by working on the land of others as agricultural labourers on daily wages, by attaching themselves to landlords, of cultivators, and as bonded labourers, and partly by pursuing their traditional 'unclean' and socially 'low' occupations of sweeping, scavenging, carrying 'nightsoil', leather work, and mat weaving.[39]

Education

Level of education is a pre-requisite to avail the constitutional safeguards especially of employment and educational reservations.[40] Only with educational advancement, and educational advancement can come about only with socio-economic advancement, their educational condition can be a crucial indicator of their overall status as beneficiaries of the implementation of the various constitutional provisions, and consequently can lay claim for a role in decision-making process.[41]

No doubt, there has been some progress in the growth of literacy among the SCs; in 1961 the literacy percentages among them and general population including them were 10.3 and 24, whereas in 1981 these were 21.4 and 36.2 respectively. Compared to the general population the increase is relatively more significant in Kerala, Himachal Pradesh, Maharashtra, Gujarat and Tamil Nadu.

Despite this increase, the SCs are still far behind the general population. This is especially so in the case of women. While the male literacy among the SCs itself is much lower than that among the general population, female literacy is much more so.

The available data might give the impression that in the primary stage the SCs have almost caught up with the general population. But, this may not be true even with a steady increase in enrolment over the years. For, enrolment is just the first step in the educational process.[42]

The report on the Programme of Action on National Educational Policy, 1986 rightly pointed out that "enrolment by itself is of little importance if children do not continue education beyond even a year, many of them not seeing the school for more than a few days". The report noted that nearly 60 percent of the children drop out between classes I-V and 75 percent between classes I-VIII and that nearly 22 percent of the enrolled at the primary stage are outside 6-11 age group, mostly overaged. For obvious reasons the corresponding percentages among the SCs must be still higher.[43]

As the SCs move up further in the educational ladder, their enrolment ratio also shrinks and their drop our rate increases correspondingly. As the first report (1978-79) of the Commission for SCs and STs noted, for a population of about 15 percent, at the all-India level the percentage of SC students in professional and other educational courses was only 4.3 in 1964-65, and only 5.7 in 1974-75. At the State level, it was only in Maharashtra that their enrolment as percentage of the total enrolment in high school, under-graduate (UG), and post-graduate (PG) equalled or exceeded their population percentage in 1976-78. In virtually all other States it was below their population percentage at all the three stages. The access of the SCs to higher education is further reduced by the fact that the instruction issued by the Government of India for reservation of seats are not followed by a number of States.

TABLE - 9
Literacy Percentage of SCs
(5 States with highest rates)

Sl. No.	States		Male			Female			Total		
			1961	1971	1981	1961	1971	1981	1961	1971	1981
1.	Kerala	SCs	31.6	74.1	62.3	17.4	33.4	49.7	24.4	40.2	56.0
		Gen.	55.0	66.6	75.3	38.9	54.3	65.7	46.8	60.4	70.4
2.	Gujarat	SCs	33.9	39.9	53.1	10.7	15.0	26.6	22.5	27.7	29.8
		Gen.	41.1	46.1	54.4	19.1	24.8	32.3	30.5	35.8	43.7
3.	Maharashtra	SCs	25.5	37.0	48.9	5.7	12.9	21.5	15.8	25.3	35.6
		Gen.	42.0	51.0	58.8	16.8	26.4	34.8	29.8	39.2	47.2
4.	Himachal Pradesh	SCs	14.5	27.4	41.9	2.0	9.7	20.6	8.5	18.8	31.5
		Gen.	27.2	43.2	53.2	6.2	20.2	31.5	17.1	32.0	42.5
5.	Tamil Nadu	SCs	23.6	32.2	40.7	5.7	11.3	18.5	14.7	21.8	29.7
		Gen.	44.5	51.8	58.3	18.2	26.9	35.0	31.4	39.5	46.8
6.	All India	SCs	17.0	22.4	31.1	3.3	6.4	10.9	10.3	14.7	21.4
		Gen.	34.5	39.5	46.9	13.0	18.7	24.8	24.0	29.5	36.2

Sources : Tabulated from Census of India, Vol.1, Parts VA(i) and IIc(i) of 1961; Series 1, Parts IIA (ii) and VA(ii) of 1971; and series 1, Part IIB (i-iii) of 1981.

Representation in Public Services

Securing an adequate representation for SCs/STs in Public Services was one of the objectives with which provision was made for reservation principle in the Constitution. But unfortunately, the scheme was not implemented in the same spirit, with the result, there is a very wide gap between the policy and the actual position obtaining today. There are several instances wherein the appointing authorities have resorted to de-reservation.[44] Moreover, taking advantage of the various weaknesses in the reservation principle, large scale misuse of the scheme by unscrupulous elements has taken place. More often than not, such instances go unnoticed, since they are not reported to the appropriate official agencies for verification and the violators go scot free.

Though the representation of SCs in the Central Services has increased over the years in all the four classes of jobs, it is only in class IV, that it has been adequate. In classes I and II, it has been far below their population percentage.

TABLE - 10
Representation of SCs in Central Services

Date	*Class 1* %	*Class 2* %	*Class 3* %	*Class 4* %	*Population* %
1-1-1960	1.2	2.5	7.2	17.2	14.7
1-1-1965	1.6	2.8	8.9	17.8	
1-1-1970	2.3	3.8	9.9	18.1	14.8
1-1-1975	3.4	5.0	10.7	18.6	
1-1-1984	6.9	10.4	14.0	20.2	15.8

Note : Corresponding population percent as per the censuses of 1961, 1971, and 1981 respectively.

Source : Government of India, Report of the Planning Commission's Working Group on SCs and STs 1980-85, Reports of the Commissioner for SCs and STs 1970-71 to 1979-81; and of the Commission for SCs and STs, 1978-79 to 1985-86.

From the foregoing, it is very clear that the nation has failed miserably in translating Ambedkar's legacy towards the Scheduled Castes and STs. The wide gap between the ideal and reality has become so wide that it is today a chasm. The tragedy is that Dr. Ambedkar's legacy which sought to operate outside Hindu religion has also not succeeded in breaking the status quo. Dr. Ambedkar felt that organisation, education and agitation would enable the *dalits* to reverse caste prejudices. As it has turned out, *dalit* political groups are totally disorganised. Education has only led to the emergence of a *dalit* elite class which has slowly distanced itself from agitational *dalit* politics. Instead of constructive agitation, *dalit* movements have either been absorbed within mainstream parties or else have degenerated into negative militancy. The deification of Dr. Ambedkar by building statues in every village appears to have taken precedence over any fight for equal rights.

There is, therefore, an urgent need to redouble our efforts to implement the precepts with more dynamism. A few suggestions in this direction are put forward.

1. There appears to be a lack of social commitment for the vigorous implementation of programmes aimed at elimination of disabilities of the SCs/STs. This condition is very necessary if any meaningful results are to be achieved. Any amount of desirable legislation will not yield worthwhile results unless

there is a real change of heart among those entrusted with the responsibility of putting into practice the legislative measures. Implementation of the measures not only in letter but in spirit is very essential. In this context, it is pertinent to recall Ambedkar's observation that "rights are protected not by law but by the social and moral conscience of society", that "if social conscience is such that is prepared to recognise the rights which law chooses to enact, rights will be safe and secure" and that if the "rights are opposed by the community, no law, no parliament, no judiciary can guarantee them in the real "sense of the word".

2. Granting statutory status to the Commission for SCs and STs will go a long way in transforming their socio-economic conditions. The high level commission that was set up in 1978 is handicapped in performing its functions effectively as it does not enjoy any constitutional status and consequently, its role is purely recommendatory which has made it at times "a helpless spectator of non-performance and non-compliance". Many of the loopholes in the implementation of the ameliorative programmes for the SCs/STs can be effectively plugged and meaningful results will be forthcoming. Fortunately, the present government seems to be thinking on those lines.

3. Formulation of imaginative and integrated long term perspective development programmes meant for the SCs/STs is another important aspect. The stupendous task of transforming their socio-economic conditions cannot be activised by adhoc and compartmentalised programmes irrespective of the huge amounts pumped into them. Though the special component plan introduced since the sixth plan was expected to fill this lacunae, so far it has not made much headway.

4. There is an urgent need for effective implementation of land reforms. Possession of land holding determines the status of an individual in society. This naturally decides the extent to which he can participate in political processes. Since the SCs/STs fall under the category of landless labour or at the most belong to the marginal farmers' group, they are marginal to the political system and weak links in the economic activities. Realising the role of land in the economic emancipation of SCs/STs the government has made concerted efforts to bring about land reforms. Though several well-intentioned legislative measures

were enacted, they have failed to achieve the desired objective either due to weaknesses in the measures or lack of will on the part of the bureaucracy for effective implementation or faulty implementation.

5. Providing adequate and meaningful security at the time of election to the SCs/STs for free exercise of their franchise is another desirable requirement. In this context it is essential that private armies maintained by landlords or upper caste groups should be banned. It is with the help of these armed lumpens that SCs/STs are practically terrorised and prevented from going to the polling booths at the time of elections and large scale rigging is resorted to by upper caste people.

6. Inculcating the ideal of casteless society in the younger generation by incorporating suitable lessons at the primary school stage will inject sanity into the caste ridden society. The children at this stage are so receptive to ideals like casteless society, observance of values like catholicity of outlook, compassion, kindness, treating the neighbours with courtesy and elders with respect, etc. An effort, therefore, should be made to teach them these concepts so that they imbue qualities which will make society more equitable and thus eliminate social frictions and tensions.

7. It is needless to mention that in order to bring quick transformation in the economic status of the SCs and STs, there is every need to enhance the allocation of funds for the relevant welfare programmes. As of now the allocation for this purpose is very meagre and woefully inadequate. During the first 30 years of planning, the SCs and STs were left out on the fringe and paltry provisions made under the sector of 'welfare of backward classes' hardly accounted for one to two percent of the total outlays. This should be raised to about six percent of the total plan outlays. If not more.

8. There is every need to strengthen the governmental machinery for enforcement of laws on untouchability and other social evils. The present machinery is found to be totally inadequate to meet this requirement resulting in their not being able to generate confidence among the SCs and STs. Consequently, those adversely affected merely approach the official agencies. This is an undesirable tendency because unless the enforcing machinery is strengthened to generate confidence in its effec-

tiveness and for the speedy disposal of grievances, the aggrieved groups may look to extremist elements or might resort to violence.

9. It is surprising that even after Independence, atrocities against the SCs and STs continue to be perpetrated. In fact, it is found that they are on the increase. The loopholes in the laws are exploited to the maximum by the perpetrators of the atrocities and go scot free. Even when cases are registered against them because of their connections with those in power succeed in avoiding punishment. They are even prepared to purchase the silence of witnesses either by inducement of economic benefits or by threats of consequences. It is, therefore, necessary that lacunae in the laws should be removed. In addition, atrocities against SCs and STs should be made non-bailable crimes. Deterrent punishment should be incorporated in the laws as punishment for such crimes. Special courts exclusively to deal with such cases must be established so that speedy trials can be ensured.

10. The composition of the police and para-military forces in the States should be changed so as to create confidence in them among the depressed classes. This can be done by inducing SCs and STs in larger number to join these forces.

To conclude, the problem of socio-economic emancipation of SCs/STs is one which does not brook any further delay. It has to be tackled with all seriousness and sincerity. Slippages of any type may create new problems and lead to social tensions which may ultimately adversely affect the social and political fabric. Also there is every danger that these sections may come under the influence of extremist groups which is to be avoided in the general interest of the country as a whole.

References

1. Government of India, *Census of India Report*, 1991.
2. Dhananjay Keer, *Dr. Ambedkar: Life and Mission.*, Bombay, Popular Prakasan., 1981, p. 392.
3. Celestin Bougle, *Essays on the Caste System*, (Translation with an Introduction by D.F. Poocock), Cambridge University Press, 1971, p.17.

4. Madhusudhan Reddy K. "Impact of Reservation Policy : Some Reflections" in Sharma B.A.V. and Madhusudhan Reddy K., (Eds.,) *Reservation Policy in India*, New Delhi, Light and Life Publishers, 1982, p. 457.
5. Dhananjay Keer, *op. cit.*
6. Eleanor Zelliot, "The Leadership of Baba Saheb Ambedkar" in Pande B.N. (ed.) *Leadership in South Asia*, New Delhi, Vikas Publishing House Pvt. Ltd., 1977.
7. Singh M.P., "Political Arrival" in *Seminar*, No. 243, November 1979, pp. 12-18.
8. Rajasekharaiah A.M., "Dr. B.R. Ambedkar on Reservation Policy" in Sharma and Madhusudhan Reddy K. (Eds.) *op.cit.*, p. 24.
9. Radhakrishnan P., "Ambedkar's Legacy to Dalits : Has the Nation Reneged on its Promise?" in *Economic and Political Weekly*, Vol. XXVI, No. 33, August 17, 1991, pp.1911-1922.
10. Radhakrishnan P., *op. cit.*
11. Barbara R. Joshi, "Ex-Untouchables : Problems, Progress and Policies in Indian Social Change" in *Pacific Affairs*, Vol. 53, No. 2, Summer 1980, p.194.
12. Rajasekharaiah, A.M., *op.cit.*, p. 24.
13. For details of this Act and its Limitations, see: *Report of the Commissioner for SCs/STs, 1971-1973, 1973-1978* and of the *Commissioner for SCs/STs for 1978-79.*
14. For the scope of this Act, see: *Report of the Commissioner for SCs/STs 1977-78* and of the *Commissioner for SCs/STs 1978-1979.*
15. *Reports of the Commissioner and the Commission for SCs/STs, 1978-79 to 1985-86.*
16. ibid.
17. Barbara R. Joshi, "Ex-Untouchables: Problems, Progress and Policies in Indian Social Change" in *Pacific Affairs*, Vol. 53, No. 2, Summer 1980, p. 194.
18. *Report of the Commissioner for SCs/STs, 8th Report*, 1985-86.
19. Barbara R.Joshi, *op.cit.*
20. See: *The Seventh Report of the Commission.*
21. Gunnar Myrdal, *Asian Drama : An Inquiry into the Poverty of Nations*, London : Allen Lane the Penguin Press, 1972, p. 276.
22. For details of the latest atrocity perpetrated by high caste Hindus against the SCs in Andhra Pradesh, see: Venkateshwara Rao M., "Tsundur's Shame : Dalits Chased and Killed in A.P. Village' in *Frontline:*, Vol. 8, No. 17, August 17-30, 1991, pp. 13-14.
23. Rajdeep Sardesai, "Atrocities on Dalits" in *Deccan Chronicle*, September 13, 1991.
24. See: Udayan Sharma (Ed.) *Violence Erupts*, New Delhi : Radhakrishna Prakashan, 1978, and Sharma K.L., "Class Stratification and Atrocities" in *Seminar*, No. 243, November 1979, pp. 22-25.
25. *Report of the Commissioner for SCs and STs.*, Eighth Report, 1985-86.
26. Rajdeep Sardesai, "Atrocities on Dalits" in *Deccan Chronicle*, September 13, 1991.
27. Radhakrishnan, P., *op. cit.*

28. *Report of the Commissioner for SCs/STs Part I, 1975-76, 1976-77*, p. 112 for an account of some typical cases of atrocities of police, see: Part II, p.49, of the above report.
29. *The Week*, Vol. 9, No. 35, August 25, 1991.
30. Barbara R.Joshi, *op. cit.*
31. *Weekend Newstime*, August 18, 1991.
32. See, Panikkar K.M., *Hindu Society at Cross Roads*, Bombay, Asia Publishing House, 1961.
33. Mumtaz Ali Khan, *Scheduled Castes and their Status in India*, New Delhi; Uppal Publishing House, 1980, p. 92.
34. Krishna Rao Y.V., "Implementation of Land Reforms in Andhra Pradesh" in Sharma B.A.V. (Ed), *The Political Economy of India*, New Delhi; Light and Life Publishers, 1980.
35. Public Accounts Committee of the Andhra Pradesh State Legislature, *Eight Report (Part II) 1981-82*.
36. Sivalinga Prasad V. and Seetha Rama Rao K., "How Land-lords Beat Ceiling Law" in *Mainstream* Vol. XIX, No. 28, March 14, 1981, pp.18-20.
37. Govt. of Andhra Pradesh, *Land Reforms in Andhra Pradesh*, Hyderabad, 1979, pp. 2-4.
38. Eleanor Zelliot, "Learning the use of Political Power : The Mahars of Maharastra" in Rajni Kothari (Ed.), *Caste in Indian Politics*. New Delhi : Orient Longman Ltd., 1973.
39. Radhakrishnan P., *op. cit.*,
40. Agaiah Chary A., "Education and Preferential Treatment Policy" in Sharma B.A.V. and Madhusudhan Reddy K. (Eds), *Reservation Policy in India*, *op.cit.*
41. Andre Beteille, "The Future of Backward Classes - The Compelling Demands of Status and Power" in *Perspective* (Supplement to the Indian Journal of Public Administration) Vol. XI, No. 1, Jan.-March 1965.
42. Abba Sayulu Y.B.,. *Sociology of Depressed Groups*, Hyderabad Centre of Harijan Studies, Osmania University, 1979, p. 40.
43. Victor D' Souza, *Educational Inequalities Among Scheduled Castes*, Chandigarh; Punjab University, 1981.
44. *Report of the Commissioner for SCs/STs 1975-76 and 1976-77*, Part I, p. 50.

6

Modernization and Loss of Livelihood for Traditional Specialists

*Dr. V.N.V.K. Sastry**

Introduction

The process of modernization in India, instead of upgrading skills of local specialists, has resulted in loss of livelihood due to displacement from these specialized fields. Another peculiar trend we observe is that the traditional specialists are neglected at macro and policy level while respected at personal level. The Constitution or Constitution makers, especially Dr. Ambedkar never wanted this to happen. In this context, a plea is made for formal recognition to traditional specialists which would not only help in modernization of traditional skills but also create mass employment for producing mass consumption of goods. This is very important for the welfare of the weaker sections, whose welfare was so dear to Dr. Ambedkar.

Traditional Specialists

The traditional specialists are broadly categorized as (i) Entertainers– (ii) Medicine-men, and (iii) Manufacturers of mass consumption goods. Let us now examine the plight of each of these groups in the context of modernization.

(i) *Entertainers* : It is everybody's knowledge that the present day famous Kuchipudi dance owes its origin to the nomadic entertainer group called Bhagavathulu hailing from Kuchapudi area in Krishna district in Andhra Pradesh. The ideas from the little tradition have been borrowed by great tradition and the facilities of modernization like flood lights, stage, public address

---

* Deputy Director, Tribal Research Institute, Hyderabad-500 028.

system etc., are used. The traditional groups still wander in the villages with torn-out clothes and empty stomachs because of reduced patronage. The skill is not lacking but the finances required for its, modernization are lacking reducing them to the stage of begger nomads. What a fall in culture.

If we examine the case of 'Dommara' community who does daring gymnastics (Acrobats) by tradition, most of their women in these families have now turned to prostitution. A few families still practising tradition have to do it in the hot sun with a high risk of falling on ground and breaking their bones. While this is so, there is a very good patronage to circus companies even though they also face competition from Cinema and Television.

One more example is that of 'Pental Dora' who wears the dress of a military man with a wooden toy gun in hand to entertain all age groups. Now-a-days, no body bothers about him. He laments, "Who will hear me after seeing entertainers in cinema"?

(ii) *Medicine-Men* : The second group of traditional specialists are medicine-men. They do not share their knowledge with others due to magico-religious aspects of medicine associated with this specialization. A large population in rural areas and especially in tribal areas still depend on native medicine. Many educated and modern men after exhausting all modern medical care normally approach native medicine-men for treatment of diseases like Paralysis, Asthma, Diabetes, Jaundice, while several allopathic doctors privately recommend for native medicine when modern medicine fails. But the condition is that we cannot give a formal recognition to this at a macro level. We appreciate the traditional medicine at individual level. Instead of accepting our ignorance of these medical practices, we brush aside the traditional medicine.

In this context, one would like to pose a question: What if a traditional Koya tribal medicine, man or a nomadic Mandula (Medicine) tribe who has a long history of treating several diseases is appointed as medical officer or lecturer in Ayurveda College? One may say that he does not have a formal degree. One's reply would be, we are not insisting on a formal degree when making appointments to posts of Principals of Music Colleges as we are offering these posts to renowned singers or musicians. How could there be a formal degree for a traditional specialisation based on informal learning. Moreover, is it not a contradiction to kill a traditional specialisation and learn the same through a formal college of Ayurveda.

(iii) *Manufacturers* : The third category of traditional specialists are manufacturing goods required for consumption by the masses. They also are losing their way of life in the process of modernisation.

A traditional cobbler is a specialist in his own field. Let us compare him with a person manufacturing shoes for Bata-shops. While the former has generations of specialisation handed over to him along with of course, the stigma attached to his occupation by the society, the latter has finances, technology and show room—all provided by modernisation.The traditional specialist is displaced and the once manufacturer is becoming 'repairer' of shoes.

Similarly, if we take the example of traditional weaver, we find that his source of livelihood is eroded by cloth produced by industry. A tribal basket maker has to steel bamboo from forest to make a living as this bamboo is given on long lease to paper mills at throw away prices. A fisherman's way of life is threatened by mechanised fishing boats.

Change in Policy Required

The modernisation has resulted in loss of livelihood to crores of traditional specialists who were serving the society in their own way. The resultant effect is unemployment. If we are to solve this problem, a radical change in industrial and educational policy is required. The manufacture of mass consumption goods like clothes, shoes etc., are to be reserved exclusively to village industries.

Introduction of modernisation to traditional skills would go a long way in meeting the changing tastes of consumers. Liberalisation of procedures in Khadi and Village Industries Boards, Nationalised Banks etc., is required similarly survival of traditional specialists is also required.

Regarding education, there could be formal education upto 7th class to make every body utilize benefits of modernisation through education. But after 7th class, there could be two streams of students. One for bright among them going for higher studies as at present and the other for learning modern skills in traditional occupations. By this it does not mean that a weaver's son has to opt for weaving or a cobbler's son has to be cobbler. But any 7th class student can opt for any trade.

For example, a student opting for weaver's occupation could learn use of power looms, modern methods of designing on cloth etc. Similarly, another student opting for fisheries could go for learning fisheries technology. Same is the case with Agriculture, Horticulture, Sericulture, etc. All this calls for a change in industrial and educational policy to create mass employment.

7

Dr. Ambedkar's Economic Philosophy : A Few Reflections

*M.S. Kallur**

Introduction

The Nation is celebrating, this year, the centenary of Dr. Babasaheb Ambedkar, one of the *Dramatis Personae* of Indian History. Dr. Bhimrao Ramji Ambedkar was born on April 14, 1891 at Ratnagiri district to a family of Mahars, the largest untouchable caste in Maharashtra. With the help of Sayajirao Gaekwad, the benevolent Maharaja of Baroda, he had the fortune of getting an education of the highest order, at a time when his fellow-men had hardly any access even to its rudiments.

Ambedkar was a versatile personality, a great nationalist, political thinker, revolutionary and reformer, chief architect of Indian Constitution, the champion of down-trodden, an economist and a prolific writer with produgious ideas. Here, an attempt is made to interpret his economic ideas from the point of their relevance to our times in the following paragraphs.

Dr. Ambedkar is not popularly noted as an economist. However, this facet of Babasaheb needs to be brought out. He was a great product of the Universities of Bombay, Columbia, London and Bonn. He was a student of two great economists of his times, Seligman and Cannon, authorities respectively on theory and taxation.[1] His well known books on economics are : "Ancient Indian Commerce", "The Evolution of Provincial Finance in British India", "Small Holdings in India and their Remedies" and "The Problem of the Rupee".

---

* Chairman, Department of Economics, Gulbarga, University, Karnataka.

Economic Philosophy

Economic philosophy is an enquiry into the fundamentals of economics like property, utility, value and so on.[2] Ambedkar's E.P. is expressed in his ideas on 'mixed economy', Socialism', 'Industrialization', 'State ownership of industries', 'Workers' right to strike' etc. As an economic thinker, he belongs to the group of 'liberal thinkers'. By and large, his orientation is that of a 'socialist', but he does not agree with Karl Marx whose ideas and methods are violent to him. One will not be wrong if he describes him as the follower of 'Keynesian Economic School'. He was, in his life time, overwhelmed by the problem of the down-trodden and one can also discern it in his economic ideas a great concern for them. He knew pretty well that these people, most of whom were *dalits*, were being exploited by landlords and capitalists and to prevent it, he suggested 'mixed economy' or 'State socialism'.

Mixed Economy

As has been mentioned above, it is nothing but his advocacy of 'State Socialism'. Far from indulging in the practise of any extreme type of 'individualism' as is practised in America or of extreme type of 'socialism' as is found, at present, in China, he rightly emphasized 'mixed economy' which does not deny the moral and spiritual foundations of human society. His concept of 'mixed economy' stresses the three economic processes of human society; (1) adaptation of the key industries and agricultural land to meet the demands of the poorer sections of society; (2) maintenance of the productive resources by the State; and (3) a just distribution of the common produce among the different people without any distinction of caste or creed.[3] We have accepted his idea of 'mixed economy' and, in fact, it is embodied in the Directive Principles of the Constitution. Now, after forty years of Independence, we are in a better position to understand his concept of 'mixed economy'; as we have come to know the defects of both 'extreme capitalism' and 'extreme socialism'. Here, Ambedkar is more relevant than Gandhi who argued for 'de-control' policy fully.[4] Further, he is not an 'Utopian Socialist'. For, by being a 'practical socialist', "he seeks to synthesize what he considers to be sound elements in both socialism and individualism and he includes them in his common good. This is derived from the supreme values of the individual and social life."[5]

The Ideal of Economic Realism

Ambedkar regards both 'capital' and 'labour' as complementary to each other. It is a realistic view. Many a technological innovations which use 'capital' have been such as would require added labour.[6] As he knew the problems realistically, he rightly opined that, "(1) Nationalisation of industries is necessary, if the interests of the public at large area is to be safeguarded adequately. This is the only way by which economic order can be profitable to all men and women with necessary provision of physical facilities to them. (2) The object of nationalisation is to better the lot of the workers. Wages should be sufficient to live happily and which also allow the development of mind, body and character. The number of the working hours should be reduced and workers be given equal pay for equal work. It is the responsibility of the State to prevent unemployment and exploitation. (3) Economic realism stands for the best utilization of natural resources.These natural resources should be conserved for the present and future happiness of all men and should not be destroyed by the individuals whose only concerns is their own private good. A Socialist State should be guided purely by consideration of service motives. (4) The idea of economic realism wishes a complete transformation of society under the new set-up. There should be unity of purpose and the principle of social usefulness, human happiness and brotherhood than personal gain..."[7] All these ideas have become very-very important to our policy makers, now. Our public sector units have already achieved the goal of bettering the lot of workers; they have regulated number of working hours and the concept of equal pay for equal work is almost fully attained in them.

While supporting the idea of 'State Socialism', he clearly says that the State control over industries should not be just for the heck of it. On the other hand, ".....main purpose behind State socialism is to put an obligation on the State to plan the economic life of the people on lines, which would lead to the highest point of productivity without closing every avenue to private enterprise, and also provide for the equitable distribution of wealth."[8] If he were alive today, he would have certainly argued for 'privatisation' of some of the lines as some of the public sector industries have not been successful in achieving the goal of 'high productivity', inspite of the fact that they have the best men and material with them. Therefore, he was rightly against complete Statization of economy and State monopoly.[9]

While being a friend of labourers in matters like 'regulation of working hours', 'bettering the lot of the workers by providing them wages sufficient to live happily' etc., he had the guts to hold the 'realistic' and 'developmental' view that, ".....the weapon of strike should be used sparingly and to the advantage of the workers and not realise political objectives of the Communist leaders..."[10]

Even now, it is the best piece of advice of him to our labourers and trade union leaders who very often go on strike for other than genuine reasons. It is an open secret that, at present, Trade Unions are under the control of political parties and these parties often misuse labourers for realisation of their selfish ends—be it a Communist party or any other party.

Ambedkar had the rational view of many concepts when compared with his contemporaries. It is said that modern machine and civilization have produced many social and economic evils in our times. This made Gandhi to oppose the introduction of 'machinery' totally at one time and by doing so he earned the title of 'medieval mystic' for himself from his critics. On the contrary, Ambedkar, a contemporary of Gandhi, harboured a rational view of machinery and modern civilisation. He says, "If the machine and modern civilisation have not benefited everybody, the remedy is not to condemn machinery and civilisation, but to alter the organisation of society so that the benefits will not be usurped by the few but will accrue to all."[11] Again, he did not mix up the 'economics' with 'religion' like Gandhi. Gandhi, based on religion gave us the impractical idea of 'trusteeship' to us.[12] On the other hand, we don't find such 'economic' ideas in Ambedkar. Perhaps, this may be due to the fact that Ambedkar wasn't only an 'economist' of international repute but also he understood the mentality of people completely.

References

1. Lewis, H. Haney, *History of Economic Thought*, Macmillan, 1957.
2. Joan Robinson, *Economic Philosophy*, Penguin Books, 1966.
3. D.R. Jatava, *The Social Philosophy of B.R. Ambedkar*, Phonies Publishing House, Agra,1965, p.117.
4. V.N. Kuber, *B.R. Ambedkar*, Publication Division, 1990, pp.12-22.
5. K.S. Bharathi, *Foundations of Ambedkar Thought*, Dattsons Publishing Co., Nagpur, 1990, p.94.
6. It is empirically proved in Punjab and Haryana, where the Green Revolution, has promoted the 'labour' use along with the use of capital. Plethora of books on Indian Agriculture explain this phenomenon.
7. D.R. Jatava, *op. cit.*, pp.126-127.
8. B.R. Ambedkar, *State and Minorities*, p.30.
9. K.S. Bharathi, *op. cit.*, p.98.
10. Dhananjay Keer, *Dr. Ambedkar, Life and Mission*, Popular Prakashan, Bombay, 1981, p.117.
11. B.R. Ambedkar, *What Congress and Gandhi Have Done to the Untouchables*, p.124.
12. For details on the concepts of 'trusteeship' as an impractical idea, refer: M.S. Kallur, "Gandhian Trusteeship: A Few Reflections", *Gulbarga University Research Journal*, Volume No. 1, June 1988, pp. 33-38.

8

Policies of Dr. Ambedkar for Uplift of Weaker Sections

*Sri Ram Murthy**

Divid-et-impera (divide and rule) policy of the British has had the grip from 18th century onwards over the Indian population to an extreme extent. Previously existing three main streams of divide viz., (1) The Aryan-Dravidian (2) Hindu-Muslim and (3) Hindu-Harijan was conveniently exploited for the purpose of stability in India by the historians. This was the time when Swami Vivekananda observed, "Your religion is in the kitchen, your Gods are in the cooking pots" and appealed "awake, arise, stop not till the goal is reached." Earlier than Swami Vivekananda, Swami Dayananda had renunciated and preached against idol-worship. Arya Samaj has realised the importance of Hindus getting united into social and political activism.

Influenced by the preachings of Guru Kabir, Dr. Ambedkar later realised that calling any one as Mahatma is meaningless since to become a human being itself is very difficult. That is why he always addressed Gandhiji not as Mahatma Gandhi but only Mr. Gandhi. The rational and secular ideas, in one way resembling to those of Lord Buddha when reflected in the poems of Kabir and they impressed Dr. Ambedkar to a large extent. Added to the social disabilities of his community, he changed his views of being a dedicated poem chanting 'Hindu' to a Hindu "fighting-against the social evils" quite early in his life. The speech he gave at the G.I.P. Railway Depressed Class Workmen's Conference at Manmad on 12th February 1938, is worth noting. He said—

---

* Principal, College of Education, Osmania University, Hyderabad - 7.

> "... The depressed classes are shut out from the weaving department in the cotton mills both in Bombay and in Ahmedabad. They can work only in the Spinning Department which is the lowest paid department. The reason why they are excluded from the weaving department is because they are untouchables and because on that account the caste Hindu worker objects to work with them although he does not mind working with the Musalmans."

The first measure he envisaged for upliftment of depressed is to inspire the depressed to oppress their self-confidence. He addressed, "If you believe in living a respectable life, you believe in self-help which is the best help. You must abolish your slavery yourself. Do not depend for its abolition by some others or God."

He continued to explain the rationality, "Your salvation lies in political power and not in making pilgrimages and observance of fasts. Devotion to scriptures would not free you from your bondage, want and poverty. Your forefathers have been doing it for generations, but there has been no respite nor even a slight difference in your miserable life in any way".

He concentrated, therefore, on a very important tool for having the depressed uplifted—the "Legislative". He concluded—"It is the duty of Legislature to provide for you (depressed) food, clothes, shelter and above all 'education'. He appealed to the masses to realise "the work of law making and of its execution". He wanted that the depressed classes should partake not only in 'Law is the abode of all worldly happiness" and therefore, accosted "You capture the power of law-making". He showed the channel very reasonably— "your duty is to divert your attention from fasting, worship and penance and apply it to capturing law-making power. It is not enough that a people are in majority numerically but they must be always watchful, strong, well-educated and self-respecting to attain and maintain success. We must shape our course ourselves and by ourselves."

Dr. Ambedkar also paid attention to the cause of women upliftment and hailed, "Never regard yourself as untouchables.

Live a clean life. Dress like the touchable ladies. Attend more to the cultivation of the mind and the spirit of self-help".

His witticism and sense of humour could be experienced subtly in his own lines "as long as the opposition cursed me, it is taken for granted that my work for you (depressed) is on the right lines. Learn to live in this world with self-respect. You should always cherish some ambition to do something in this world for they alone rise who strive".

Dr. Ambedkar in his constructive ordeal recommended to the Minorities Committee of the Round Table Conference that "before majority rule is established their (depressed) emancipation from the system of untouchability must be an accomplished fact. The depressed classes must be made free citizens entitled to all the rights of citizenship in common with other citizens of the State".

Before proceeding further about Dr. Ambedkar's policies for uplift of weaker sections it is worth noting his views about the 'Politics' and its future in functioning due to the impact of 'Caste System'. He observed that "voting is always communal. The voter votes for the candidate of his community and not for the best candidate. Thus, the majority community win the seat by the sheer communal majority".

"The minority community is forced to vote for the candidate of majority community. The votes of minority community are not enough to enable the candidate to win the seat against the candidate put up by the majority community. As a consequence, the votes of the majority community can never condemn to give his vote to a candidate of a minority community. On the other hand, the voter of the minority community who is socially on a lower level takes pride in giving his vote to the candidate of the majority community".

That is how a minority community candidate always gets defeated in election. This aspect has worked as an eye opener and remedial steps were envisaged later in free India for obtaining representation essentially from all categories of the society. This is also considered as a major step of policy for the upliftment of depressed since the voice from them is heard through the representative who necessarily has to partake in the highest bodies of policy-making. Here Dr. Ambedkar paid rich tributes to Mahatma Jyotiba Phule (1827-1890) by dedicating his book "Who were the Shudras?" to him. While dedicating the book he inscribed "to the Memory of Mahatma Jyothiba Phule, the greatest Shudra of modern India who made the lower classes of Hindus conscious of their slavery to the higher classes and who preached the gospel that for India *Social Democracy* was more vital than *independence from foreign rule*".

The main salient features of Dr. Ambedkar's policies are worth consolidating for more absorption:

1. Like all other religions, only one book should be prescribed for all Hindus that is acceptable to them and no doctrine, religious or social, contained in Vedas, Shastras and Puranas be prescribed as sacred or authoritative.

2. All priests must be appointed to temples after successfully going through an examination and obtaining a certificate. A priest who does not hold the certificate cannot perform any ceremony and if did so should be treated as invalid by the law of the nation.

3. Morals, beliefs and worship should be paid utmost attention and by treating priest as the servant of the State, necessary disciplinary action should be taken by the State if necessary.

4. The number of priests should be limited by law and the group must be brought under control by legislation.

Thus, the monopoly of the particular caste and the ability of such people to exploit others through religion, could be controlled.

Dr. Ambedkar opposed the use of force or compulsion to promote social integration. He says, "The State is both the child and the parent of law. There is the law which governs the State and the law by means of which the State governs".

Dr. Ambedkar's vision is so sharp that he observed, "Society can practice tyranny and oppression against an individual in a far greater degree than a government can—What punishment in the penal code is comparable in its magnitude and in its severity to ex-communication?

By getting perturbed with the level of untouchability practised among Hindus he appealed to the Scheduled Castes ultimately to change their religion. He observed that those who become Muslims and Christians are not treated by the Hindus as untouchables and will not be discriminated against and will not be treated unequally. Thus, he appealed the Scheduled Castes to become Buddhists. He declared, "To reform the Hindu society is not our aim. We want our independence and that is our aim".

Gandhiji considered Dr. Ambedkar's decision as an unfortunate one. He believed in the eternal unity of Hinduism and apparently continued to work for it by offering appropriate compensation for the shameful persecution to which the vast mass of Harijans are exposed in his later part of life.

In the last part of his life Dr. Ambedkar felt the vacuum that is likely to exist after his departure and said that, "I wanted that somebody from the Scheduled Castes should come forward and take the responsibility from me. There, however, seems none to shoulder such a heavy responsibility, all are selfish and quarrel among themselves on petty matters. I have not been able to fulfil my mission. I wanted to do more for the Scheduled Caste people and to see them as a governing class in my life".

Later by understanding the importance of Dr. Ambedkar's mission various political leaders have taken up the issue and continued the struggle for uplifting the depressed classes and at the same time maintaining the unity of Hindus. Yet the task remains crucial and lot has to be done because the provisions that are made through legislation are not foolproof.

Epilogue

The vertical expansion of the major legislated provision i.e. "Reservation" has to be controlled and be made available to the masses in a horizontal manner. What we mean here is that every depressed class individual must be given a chance to join the mainstream of life, through the provision of reservation, which becomes impossible when one who enjoys the facility of reservation at many stages of life. This could be thoroughly understood when we observe in education, the behaviour of a first generation child compared to a second generation child who had the facilitated environment during the childhood by virtue of his family or parents being educated. As the percentage of reservations are limited for horizontal application that commemmorate the total number of depressed individual is not possible. And thus, some solution must be sought to see that the horizontal expansion is accelerated so that the entire depressed class group in India is benefited.

One more suggestion that is worth considering for implementation is to provide reservation only to those who cut short the social distance by virtue of marrying a person belonging to lower castes than theirs. This will reduce the hierarchy of caste system and will accelerate the removal of caste system in a two-way manner.

Finally, another suggestion that could be thought over is to provide reservations upto the first generation children at all levels of education and employment and then to do away the reservation for the children of subsequent generations after certain level of education and employment while substituting with the financial help for enabling them to compete with the remaining strata of the society.

In conclusion, however, the main-streaming, i.e., to keep the depressed class children irrespective of their generations, in the regular social strata is a must, and common activities that proliferate the uplift in all directions of the depressed should be made as the essential curriculum. Final feeling should be that we are all 'Indians' and not any individual belonging to a particular creed or caste or state.

9

Dr. Ambedkar on Indian Monetary System

*Dr. (Smt.) C.K. Degaonkar**

Dr. Ambedkar's views on Indian Monetary System are expressed clearly in his dissertation on *The Problem of Indian Rupee* which he submitted to London University for the award of D.Sc. Degree. It touches at the basic root of the problem of Indian rupee i.e. the instability in its value. It has special significance in the present period specially when Rupee is losing significantly both its internal as well as external value.

To analyse his comments and issues on Indian Monetary System it is essential to analyse the brief history of Indian currency. *The Problem of Indian Rupee* covers, the history of Indian currency till 1923. It begins with the Currency Act of 1835 in which Indian silver rupee having the weight of 180 grams of silver was made legal tender with free coinage. The silver standard continued to operate smoothly till 1874 but thereafter the adverse change in silver-gold exchange ratio made it difficult to operate it. It specially increased the burden on the Government for payment of home charges. The Government was forced to bring a reform of currency. The Herschell Committee and the subsequent Coinage Act of 1893 could not solve the problem and stabilise the exchange rate. During this period, the Government of India submitted a plan for the adoption of Gold Standard. The Fowler Committee (1898) was then appointed to suggest the measures in this regard. The committee recommended some sort of bimetallic standard and opening of a gold mint to coin sovereigns to prepare a base for gold standard. These recommendations could not be implemented due to the unwillingness of the Brit-

* Leader, Department of Economics, Sulbarga University, Sulbarga, Karnataka State.

ish Government to open a gold mint in India. This resulted in adoption of gold exchange standard, in which the rupee-sterling exchange ratio was to be maintained through the sale of council bills. The gold exchange standard created differences between the Government of India and the Secretary of the State. The Chamberlain Commission was therefore appointed to give its recommendations. It considered that active circulation of gold was not essential in India, for working of gold standard, nor the people were anxious about it. The committee was therefore in favour of gold exchange standard as it was more suitable for the country and had maintained the stability in exchange value of the rupee. The committee was also against the circulation of gold in India. The arguments extended to cover, firstly, Indian people will heard gold. Secondly, India is too poor a country to maintain such an expensive money material. Thirdly, transactions of the people are too small to permit the circulation of gold, and paper currency is most economical and popular in India.

The First World War delayed the implementation of these recommendations. The existing currency system in the post-war was different from the recommendations of the Fowler Committee. The question therefore was whether to revive it or to regularise it. Hence, the Smith Committee was appointed in 1919 to ensure the gold exchange standard. But as India faced the adverse balance of trade and this clubbed with the high domestic prices aggravated the balance of payments situation. The exchange rate fell down considerably. This led to the appointment of Hilton Young Commission in 1925, which recommended for gold bullion standard that was in practice till Independence.

This brief history of Indian currency in pre-Independence period indicates the various phases through which Indian currency has passed. Dr. Ambedkar in his *"The Problem of Indian Rupee"* established and proves the hypothesis that how the stability of the rupee remained a problem throughout the period though various reforms were undertaken. This is proved with rich statistical facts and logical analysis. The basic line of argument rests on the fact that instability is largely attributed to the most native of currency principles i.e. the requirement of the public. He draws very radical conclusions in this regard. The thesis was returned as the "exposition gave offence to British imperialist examiners who asked him to rewrite it without changing its conclusions[1]".

He stresses on the most neglected period in Indian currency from 1800 to 1893 which is essential in analysing the adoption of gold exchange standard in India. The gold exchange standard, he argues is not originally the standard suggested by the Government of India[2].

He clearly establishes his stand different from that of Keynes in this regard, to quote. "The difference proceeds from the fundamental fact which seems to be overlooked by Prof. Keynes that nothing will stabilise the rupee unless we stabilise its general purchasing power[3]."

To analyse the fact that Indian rupee could not attain stability though it underwent various reforms and this resulted in causing injustice and hardship to the masses through price variations, he develops a logical chain of thinking beginning from the Currency Act of 1835. The Act which led to silver monometallism did not consider stability but popular preference as the deciding factor in the choice of the standard metal. But this proved to be a measure inadequate to the needs of the country. At that time India was in transition period from kind to cash economy, the trade was increasing and the demand for cash also increased but the currency did not expand much as after 1850, the production of silver did not keep pace with the needs of the world economy though the paper currency was introduced partly in 1861 but the division of the country into circles, the high denomination of paper currency and lack of universal encashability made it less popular. The system therefore failed to provide stability.

After the 1870s, the silver standard failed to operate smoothly for dislocation of its parity with gold. Thus, he largely attributes to the de-monetisation of silver after 1873. Though decline in the value of silver in terms of gold had a favourable impact on India's foreign trade, but it resulted in increasing the prices in the domestic market causing a change in distribution of income in favour of the rich. Here he remarks aptly, "Very little can be said in favour of a standard which changes in its value and which becomes a via-media of transferring wealth from the relatively poor to relatively rich"[4].

Dr. Ambedkar had an unfavourable view of the gold exchange standard. The Chamberlain Commission reported that during the period of this standard in India, the trade and industry developed. The Smith Committee also supported the exchange standard. But Dr. Ambedkar held a view that trade is no doubt dependent on good money but the growth of trade is not a conclusive proof that money is good. Commerce can increase even when the currency is bad which is supported by Indian experience during 1873-93.[5]

According to him, a sound currency system should be able to maintain its value in terms of gold. The fluctuations in the value of rupee in 1893, 1900, 1907, 1914, 1917 and 1920 clearly indicate the instability of the value of the rupee. The official explanation for this was that it was due to an adverse balance of trade which was also supported by Keynes. But he says that the only scientific explanation for this is that the rupee had lost it's general purchasing power though the Smith Committee was expected to provide a solution to Indian currency problem, it did not take into consideration the general purchasing power of the rupee as a factor in stabilising the value of Indian rupee. The reason for the fall in purchasing power of the rupee is due to excess issue of the currency.

In the long run it is the general purchasing power of a currency that ultimately governs its exchange value. The price trends in Indian market after the mint closure in 1893 were not considered by any commission, including Prof. Keynes in his *"Treatise on Indian Currency and Finance"*. If the Chamberlain Commission had taken them into account it would not have recommended for gold exchange standard. If the stability of purchasing power is a criterion then one would prefer gold standard to gold exchange standard.

Searching the root of instability of the Indian rupee, he maintains that, it is due to the instability of it's purchasing power caused by undue expansion of the currency. The plan suggested by Government of India for adoption of gold currency was a better plan. The Fowler Committee, it was interested in introducing gold standard in India would have recommended for absolute stopping of the coinage of rupees and holding the Government from giving rupees for gold in failing to do so, it not only deprived the country of a sound currency system but helped to place the Indian currency on the basis of an inconvertible rupee. The Provision introduced by Herschell Committee and upheld by Fowler Committee that Government will give rupees for gold and in the absence of the counter provision that Government will give gold for rupee, it gave an authority to the Government to issue convertible rupee currency of unlimited legal tender which led to undue expansion of currency resulting in its instability of value.

His proposal for reform of Indian currency consists of—

(1) stop the coinage of rupee by absolutely closing the mints to the government as they are to the public.

(2) open a gold mint for the coinage of a suitable gold coin.

(3) fix a ratio between gold coin and rupee.

(4) rupee not to be convertible into gold and gold not to be convertible in rupees but both to circulate as unlimited legal tender at the ration fixed by law."[6]

To him the ideal currency should have two basic characteristics—stability and elasticity. It should expand with the needs of growing trade and industry at the same time, should maintain stability of value.

The emphasis on stability is a more practical view about a currency system. The stability of Indian rupee is a problem even today which has thus historical roots. Therefore, he is more practical and foresighted in this regard. His plan of reform of currency though seemed to be radical at that time would have perhaps granted the stability to the currency and would have placed Indian currency and trade on a better footing.

References

1. Kher D., Dr. Ambedkar : Life and Mission, Popular Prakashan, Bombay, 1990.
2. Government of Maharashtra, Education Department *Dr. Babasaheb Ambedkar - Writing and Speeches,* Vol. VI, Bombay, 1989. p. 327.
3. *Ibid.,* p. 328.
4. *Ibid.,* p. 439.
5. *Ibid.,* p. 505.
6. Dr. Ambedkar B.R., Statement of Evidence to the Royal Commission on Indian Currency - in *Dr. Babasaheb Ambedkar, Writings and Speeches,* Vol. VI. Government of Maharashtra, Bombay 1989, p. 630.

10

Ambedkar—Architect of The Indian Constitution

*R. Jaganmohan Rao**

Bharat Ratna Dr. Ambedkar made the posterity to remember him by his significant contribution as Chairman of the Drafting Committee of the Constitution. The present Constitution is the result of the collective wisdom and effort of Dr. Ambedkar and stalwarts like Sir B.N. Rao, Sri Alladi Krishnaswamy and many more persons. He wanted a strong democratic India. This is reflected from the provisions of the Constitution.

The Government of India Act 1935 was the step towards the evolution of democratic frame of government in India. Elections were held for the Provincial Assemblies in 1937. However, due to the outbreak of Second World War, the Provincial Legislative Assemblies were dissolved, as the Congress ministers resigned in protest against the British refusal to announce the war aims and objectives. The Viceroy inducted Dr. Ambedkar into his executive council as a member of it in 1942. Due to rapid turn of events in the world around, Labour Party headed by Lord Atlee came to power in England.The new Government in Britain sent a Cabinet Mission to India.[1] The Cabinet Mission's proposals were accepted by all leaders in India. The Cabinet Mission suggested the constitution of an Advisory Committee and four sub-committees to assist the Advisory Committee in the preparation of the Constitution. The Sub-Committees are—

(i) Fundamental Rights Committee.

(ii) Minorities Sub-Committee.

---

* Professor of Law and Principal, Andhra University College of Law, Visakhapatnam —530 003 (A.P.).

(iii) North East Frontier and Tribal Areas and Assam Excluded and Partially Excluded Areas Sub-Committee.

(iv) Excluded and Partially Excluded Areas (other than those in Assam) Sub-Committee.

Dr. Ambedkar was chosen as the Chairman of the Drafting Committee of the Indian Constitution. He played a key role, as the Chairman, and made a significant contribution to the framing of the Indian Constitution.[2] He laboriously worked for 141 days on the reports submitted by the various sub-committees.[3] In this regard he received the necessary help and advice from eminent and great stalwarts like Sir B.N. Rao, the Constitutional Adviser and Sri Alladi Krishnaswami and a host of others.[4] The greatness of Baba Saheb Ambedkar can be understood by looking at the way in which he conducted the proceedings of the Drafting Committee in reconciling the conflicting views expressed in the Constituent Assembly while piloting the Draft Constitution.

The Draft Constitution highlighted the need for adoption of the following fundamental features—

Federal Structure

Dr. Ambedkar, keeping in view the vastness of our country and diversity in language and culture of our people, stressed the need for adopting a federal structure of the government. The unique feature of our Constitution is that it is a federal State with a leaning towards central dominance in certain matters. The Constitution envisaged the creation of a dual polity consisting of the Union Government at the Centre and the States at the periphery, each endowed with sovereign powers to be exercised in the areas that are assigned to them in the Constitution. Each State has certain rights in its domain which is expected to be exercised without coming into clash with the Centre whose sphere of activity and operation are well demarcated in the Constitution.

Ambedkar tried to effect a balance between the Centre and States. This is indicated by the elaborate scheme of distribution of powers indicated in the Constitution. He believed federalism means a dual polity with the Union at the Centre and the States at the periphery, each endowed with sovereign powers to be exercised in the field assigned to them respectively by the Constitution. According to him, federalism does not mean a league of small States united in a lose relationship, nor are the agencies of the Union Government deriving powers from it. Both the Union and State Governments derive their authority from the Constitution. No State is subordinate to the Union in respect of powers allotted to it under the Constitution. They have to act in coordination with each other in order to provide larger liberties and mutual facilities for the people.[5]

Ambedkar considered the criticism that there is too much centralisation and the States have been reduced to municipalities as one based on misunderstanding. He observed[6]—

"...the basic principle of federalism is that the legislature and executive authority is partitioned between the Centre and the States not by any law to be made by the Centre but the Constitution itself. This is what the Constitution has done. The States are in no way dependent, but an inter-dependence that creates harmony, order of progress and prosperity. It looks almost contradictory in appearance, but it is the essence of federalism, and any federalism can provide such an effect. Unity while showing diversity, oneness while providing for diversion, is the outstanding characteristic of modern federalism".[7]

He considered that a federal State as an institutional means for the solution of human affairs. The Constitution has adopted a mid-way between centralisation and de-centralisation of power for the reason that[8]—

1. there is a clear demarcation of governmental powers between the Centre and the States,
2. each government is independent of the other in its own field,
3. the Constitution has provided for an independent judiciary for settling disputes between the Union and the States in respect of division of powers.

Ambedkar's concept of federalism means that State is a federation in normalcy but unitary in contingency. To him the word 'Indian Union' means—

1. that the Indian federation is not the result of an agreement by the units.

2. that the component units have no freedom to secede from it.

He firmly believed that India should be a strong nation capable of tackling the people together irrespective of State loyalties. He believed in the wisdom of the people and hoped that the federal structure in working will lead to emotional integration and national unity.

The Constitution of India though a federal one in normal times, exhibits unitary features to tide over situations created in times of war or political crisis due to constitutional breakdown.[9] In such situations, the entire federal structure gets transformed into unitary structure concentrating all powers in the Centre.[10] Ambedkar did signal service in providing for single judiciary, uniformity in laws and common All India Civil Service, all of which are essential for the unity of the country.[11]

Parliamentary Democracy

Dr. Ambedkar was a strong advocate of parliamentary form of government right from the inception of Government of India Act of 1935. He believed in the peaceful democratic methods of legislation, persuasion, discussion, concensus etc. as the most appropriate means for achieving socio-economic change. He firmly believed that the parliamentary system of government alone can usher in an egalitarian society though the application of principles of social democracy such as socio-economic justice and equality amongst the people.

Dr. Ambedkar was of the view that the essential pillars for the successful functioning of parliamentary system of government are—

(i) for the successful functioning of the democracy, active functional opposition is required. Responsible and competent opposition party is the key to a free political life. No democracy can function successfully without such an opposition party.

(ii) the second pillar of parliamentary democracy is free and fair elections. In the absence of these two pillars of democracy or in the absence of any one of these, democracy degenerates into mobocracy and dictatorship in the name of democratic form of government.

The Preamble of our Constitution echoes the principles of parliamentary democracy. It reads—

We, the PEOPLE OF INDIA, having solemnly resolved to constitute India into a SOVEREIGN (SOCIALIST SECULAR)[12] DEMOCRATIC REPUBLIC and to secure to all its citizens—

> JUSTICE, social, economic and political;
>
> LIBERTY of thought, expression, belief, faith and worship;
>
> EQUALITY of status and of opportunity; and to promote among them all;
>
> FRATERNITY assuring the dignity of the individual and the unity (and integrity)[13] of the nation.

Pandit Jawaharlal Nehru, our first Prime Minister emphasized the above principles while presenting a resolution on the Aims and Objectives of the newly adopted Draft Constitution, before the Constituent Assembly. He further urged the House to adopt the resolution without any protest or amendment.

Dr. Ambedkar, though conscious of the inherent defects in a parliamentary democracy, preferred it as the best model suitable to conditions in India. The major weaknesses of this system is that essential changes like the realisation of social and economic justice and equality cannot be expedited and promises made could be fulfilled only at a slow pace. This naturally leads to the discontentment and unrest among the people who may in turn revolt against the system and resort to violent methods. Therefore, watchful, vigilant public opinion, and effective implementation of laws and responsible executive, committed legislature, and impartial judiciary are very much essential to the success of Parliamentary democracy. Hence, Baba Saheb Ambedkar sounded a note of warning many a time that if parliamentary democracy fails to bring socio-economic justice, the result would be anarchy, rebellion and blood-shed.[14] In particular, the plight of the weaker sections—the poorest of the poor, will have to be immediately attended to. Then only the fruits of democracy can be realised. Thus, Ambedkar was very much against dictatorship and all forms of force and coercion, would only welcome democratic form of government despite its drawbacks.

Dr. Ambedkar, after pointing out the pitfalls of democracy, made some certain positive suggestions for its successful working. They are—

(i) Every democratic form of government aiming at the welfare of all people must not allow dynastic rule or hereditary authoritarian, autocratic rule to grow under its umbrella of welfare and well being of the people. The government should always struggle for the common good of all its citizens of the country irrespective of caste, creed, religion or region.

(ii) The presence of a responsible and equally committed opposition party to act as a check on the excessive, authoritarian, autocratic tendencies of an otherwise well formulated democratic form of government.

(iii) The adoption of the principle of equality, equal treatment in administrative, legislative matters, equal protection of laws must be the heart and soul of any successful government.

(iv) He strongly believed that democracy—whether the Parliamentary or Presidential form, Federal or Unitary type, or both mixed up together, would only survive when healthy conventions based on moral principles are evolved. No democratic form of government shall survive, without observing the principles of constitutional morality, such as fair method of election, with honesty and integrity etc.

Constitutional morality would also mean an effective coordination between conflicting interests of different people and the administrative cooperation to resolve them amicably without any confrontation amongst the various groups working for the realisation of their ends at any cost. For Ambedkar, moral fabric of the society, governed as well as the governance must be strong. In other words, public conscience, moral order and constitutional morality-ethics of politicians, that constitute the core of policy making, must be very sound and strong if democracy is to survive for long period of progress and prosperity for the common people.

Fundamental Rights

Part III of our Constitution guarantees the fundamental rights to the citizens/persons against the State. The novel feature of this Part is[15]—

1. These are the rights against the Central Government, Parliament, State Government and State Legislature, Local, and other authorities within the territory of India (Art. 12).
2. Some of the rights contained in Articles 15(2), 17, 23 and 24 are also enforceable against the individuals as they are very significant rights relating to the prohibition of "discrimination on grounds of religion, race, caste, sex or place of birth, forced labour and employment etc."

In addition to these, the Constitution guarantees certain other rights keeping in view the peculiar socio-economic conditions of our country. These provisions and certain others significantly reflect the intention of the framers of the Constitution to put an end to the exploitation of the down-trodden, the depressed and suppressed communities in India.[16]

National leaders like Mahatma Gandhi, Jawaharlal Nehru and Dr. Ambedkar, being influenced by Western ideals of 'Equality and Egalitarianism', of Rousseau and John Stuart Mill, rejected the basis of Hindu orthodoxy and preached the gospel of equality in national movement.[17]

Ambedkar espousing the cause of backward classes declared that caste inequality is man made rather than ordained by God. It was mainly because of his dramatisation of the cause of depressed classes the constitutional framers included the policy of compensatory discrimination.[18] Explaining the significance of including Article 16(4), he said[19]—

"The Drafting Committee has taken (all) the care to safeguard the principles of equality of opportunity, and at the same time to satisfy the demand of communities which have been not represented in the service under the State."

During the deliberations on the passage of Part III of the Constitution, Dr. Ambedkar said[20]—

"... the most criticized part of the Constitution is that which relates to fundamental rights. It is said that Article 13 (now Article 19) which deals with Fundamental Freedoms, is riddled with so many exceptions that the exceptions have eaten up the rights altogether. It is condemned as a kind of deception. In the opinion of critics, fundamental rights are not fundamental unless they are also absolute rights". Further, it is said that the fundamental rights in the American Bill of Rights are real because they are not subjected to limitations or exceptions.

"I am sorry to say that the whole criticism is based on misconception. It is incorrect to say that the fundamental rights are absolute while non-fundamental rights are not absolute. The real distinction between the two is that non- fundamental rights are the gift of the law, and the fundamental rights are the gift of the Constitution which has got every authority, interest of the State or its people to qualify them."

The most significant feature of the fundamental rights chapter is that these rights are made 'justiciable'. The right to move the Supreme Court for enforcement of fundamental rights under Article 32 is itself a fundamental right. Article 32 authorises the Supreme Court to not only issue directions, orders, or writs in the nature of Habeas Corpus, Mandamus, Certiorari etc. or any other appropriate remedy, as the case may be, for the enforcement of fundamental rights guaranteed by the Constitution. These Constitutional remedies are similar to those suggested by Dr. Ambedkar in Clause I of Section II. Without Art. 32 the insertion of Fundamental Rights in the Constitution would have become meaningless as rights are real only if they are accompanied by remedies.[21] Explaining the importance of Art. 32 he observed[22]—

"I am very glad that the majority of those who spoke on this Article have realised the importance and significance of this Article....without which Article, the Constitution would be a nullity...It is the very soul of the Constitution and the very heart of it and I am glad that the House had realised its importance."

Directive Principles

One of the distinctive features of the Indian Constitution is the enunciation in Part IV, what are called Directive Principles of State Policy. In the interim report submitted to the Constitutent Assembly, a distinction was made between fundamental rights which would be justiciable and the Directive Principles which would not be. During the course of debates in the Constituent Assembly there was a move to do away with this distinction and made them all justiciable. However, this could not be done, and distinction between the two remained. Dr. Ambedkar explained the scope of Directive Principles as follows[23]—

"The Directive Principles are like the instruments of instructions which were issued to the Governor General and the Governors of Colonies, and to those of India, by the British Government under the Government of India Act 1935. What is called 'Directive Principles' is merely another name for the instruments of instructions. The only difference is that they are instructions to the legislature and the executive. Whoever captures power will not be free to do what he likes with it. In the exercise of it he will have to respect these instruments of instructions which are called Directive Principles."

Refuting the criticism, that whatever be the ethical or political value of the Directive Principles, they have no place in a Constitution because they are only pious declarations, Ambedkar observed that[24]—

"... the Directive Principles of State Policy may not be enforceable in a court of law, but the principles laid down therein are the essence of egalitarianism, and hence are equally fundamental as the Centre and the States are directed to apply them in the actual governance of the country in order to usher in the new social and economic order in India."

Further, he said that[25] "... the Directive Principles of State Policy have no legal force behind them. I am prepared to admit it. But I am not prepared to admit that they have no sort of binding force at all. Nor am I prepared to admit that they have no sort of binding force at all. Nor am I prepared to concede that they are useless because they have no binding force in law..."

Dr. Ambedkar in conclusion on Part IV of the Constitution said[26]—

"In enacting this part of the Constitution, the Assembly is giving certain directions to the future legislature and future executive to show in what manner they are to exercise the legislative and the executive powers they will have. Surely it is not the intention to introduce in this part these principles as mere pious declarations. It is the intention of the Assembly that in future both the legislature and the executive should not merely pay lip service to these principles but they should be made the basis of all legislative and executive action .... in the matter of governance of the country".

According to Ambedkar,[27] "the Directive Principles have a great value for they lay down that our ideal is economic democracy. Because we do not want merely a parliamentary form of government...through the mechanism provided in the Constitution, without any direction as to what our social order ought to be, we deliberately included the Directive Principles in our Constitution....our object in framing this Constitution is really two fold—

(i) to lay down the form of political democracy.

(ii) to lay down that our ideal is economic democracy and also to prescribe that every Government whatever it is in power, shall strive to bring about economic democracy".

Position of the President

Dealing with the question what the position of the President under the Indian Constitution is, Dr. Ambedkar said that "...the President of India occupies the same position as the King under the English Constitution. He is the Head of the State but not of the executive. He represents the Nation, but does not rule the Nation."[28] These words of the founding father of the Constitution make it clear that the President is the titular Head and the Prime Minister is the real head who really rules the country in the sense of the term. What he means is that the President is only the Constitutional head of the State, and the Prime Minister is the *de facto* head of not only the Council of Ministers, but also of the entire country. The real power, therefore, rests in the Prime Minister.

The debates in the Constituent Assembly and speeches made therein bear ample proof to the sagacity and states-manship of Dr. Ambedkar. His invincible spirit is all pervading in the shaping of the Constitution of this great country. He is unquestionably a great scholar and a great Parliamentarian. He has been rightly chosen to discharge the duties as Chairman of Drafting Committee of the Constitution in the company of the galaxy of stalwarts like Sri Alladi Krishnaswami Ayyar, K.M. Munshi, N. Gopalaswamy Ayyangar and B.N. Rao and a host of others. His choice as Chairman and his work was hailed by no less person than the first President of India Dr. Rajendra Prasad, who also happened to be President of the Constitutent Assembly. He aptly observed[29]—

"Sitting in the Chair and watching the proceedings from day to day, I have realised as no body else could have, with what zeal and devotion the members of the Drafting Committee, especially its Chairman Dr. Ambedkar, inspite of his indifferent health, have worked (cheers). We would never make a decision which was or could be ever so right as when we put him on the Drafting Committee and made him its Chairman. He has not only justified his selection but has added lustre to the work which he has done."

Late Prime Minister Jawaharlal Nehru, while paying a glowing tribute to Dr. Ambedkar in the Lok Sabha upon his death on December 6, 1956, also said[30] that "Dr. Ambedkar played a 'most important part' in the framing of India's Constitution." In fact he added, "Dr. Ambedkar had played a very constructive role in the making of the Constitution even before his election to the Drafting Committee." Thus, to quote Nehru again, "No one took greater trouble and care over Constitution–making than Dr. Ambedkar."

The Constitution of India has sustained all these years and passed through critical and turbulent periods in the history of our nation. The Constitution is not bad and unworkable, it is the men who are incharge of it that matters. Dr. Ambedkar aptly said in similar vein[31]—

"I feel that it is workable, it is flexible, and it is strong enough to hold the country together both in peace time and war time. Indeed if I may say so, if things go wrong under the new Constitution, the reason will not be that we had a bad Constitution, what we have to say is that man was vile."

References

1. The Cabinet Mission consisted of Lord Pethic Lawrence, Sir Stafford Crips and Mr. A.V. Alexandar.
2. D.C. Ahir, *Dr. Ambedkar and Indian Constitution*, Buddha Vihar, 1973, Lucknow, pp. 33-34.
3. *Ibid.*, p. 37.
4. Drafting Committee consisted of Dr. Ambedkar as Chairman and six other members namely N. Gopalaswami Ayyangar, Alladi Krishna Swamy Ayyar, Saiyed Mohd. Sadulla, K.M. Munshi, B.C. Mitter and D.P. Khaitan (N. Madhava Rao and T.T. Krishnamachari were appointed in place of B.C. Mitter and D.P. Khaitan respectively) and B.N. Rao was the Constitutional Advisor.
5. M.V. Pyle: *Constitution of India*, p. 267.
6. *Ibid.*
7. *Ibid.*
8. *Ibid.*, p. 269
9. D.C. Ahir, *op. cit.*, p. 45.
10. *Ibid.*, pp. 50-51.
11. *Ibid.*
12. Constitution (Forty Second Amendment) Act 1976 added the words 'Socialist and Secular'.
13. Similarly for the words, "Unity of the Nation" the words "Unity and Integrity of the Nation" were substituted.
14. This reminds us about the recent revolutionary changes that have taken place in the various countries in Eastern Europe. In Romania and Poland there is a mass upsurge leading to liberalisation of political set up and ending up of one party rule. Similarly, East and West Germany united to become one German State.
15. D.C. Ahir, *op. cit.*, p. 43.
16. *Ibid.*
17. Paramanand Singh *Equality, Reservations and Discrimination*, Deep & Deep Publications, New Delhi, p.10.
18. *Ibid.*
19. *Constituent Assembly Debates*, Vol. VII, PP. 701-702.
20. *Ibid.*, pp. 40-41.
21. D.C. Ahir, *op. cit.*, p. 93.
22. *Constituent Assembly Debates*, Vol. VII, p. 93.
23. *Ibid.*, pp. 41-42.
24. *Ibid.*
25. *Ibid.*
26. *Ibid.*, p. 476.

27. D.C. Ahir, *op. cit.*, pp.101-102, *Constituent Assembly Debates*, Vol. VII, pp. 494-495.
28. *Ibid.*, p. 39.
29. *Constituent Assembly Debates*, Vol. XI, p. 994.
30. D.C. Ahir *op. cit.*, pp. 176-177.
31. *Ibid.*, p. 61.

11

Dr. Ambedkar—A Saviour of Indian Women

*Dr. P. Malyadri**

In the present crisis of the world system, in which inequalities have increased among and within nations as well as among different social groups and households, it is time to work towards seeking an alternative vision of development. In the contemporary world where heightened political tensions and increasing inequalities influence the whole of the population in many countries, women are more acutely and directly affected. They themselves need to take an active role in development priorities and outlining the parameters of a new society. Centuries rolled down in Indian civilization and unheeded plight of women touched the heart of many social revolutionaries—Dr. Ambedkar was one of them.

Dr. Ambedkar championed the cause of women as well as the miserable plight of Scheduled Castes and Scheduled Tribes throughout his career. He discussed a number of problems of Indian women and sought for their solutions in Bombay Legislative Council, in the Viceroy's Executive Council, as a Labour Member, in the Constituent Assembly as the Chairman of the Drafting Committee and also in the Parliament as the first Law Minister of Independent India.

Dr. Ambedkar was sworn in as a nominated member of the Bombay Legislative Council on 18th February, 1927. He regularly participated in the Legislative debates and also delivered a number of speeches on the budget, education, Panchayat, local boards and industries. He advised Indians to participate in the World War on behalf of the British Government. His arguments

---

* Faculty Member in Commerce, Vivekananda Government College, Vidyanagar, Hyderabad-44.

on the Maternity Benefit Bill and on Birth Control were quite relevant to recognize the dignity of women. He vehemently supported the maternity bill. His argument was—

> "It is in the interest of the nation that the mother ought to get a certain amount of rest during the pre-natal period and also subsequently, and the principle of the Bill is based entirely on that principle...."
>
> "That being so Sir, I am bound to admit that the burden of this ought to be largely borne by the Government, I am prepared to admit this fact because the conservation of the people's welfare is primary concern of the Government. And in every country, therefore, where maternity benefit has been introduced, you will find that the Government has been subjected to a certain amount of charge with regard to maternity benefit".[1]

Apart from this, Dr. Ambedkar argued, that the employer should not be free from the liability. It is absolutely reasonable to state that the employer gets certain special benefits by employing women instead of men. Further, Dr. Ambedkar thought that this bill should not be confined to the Bombay Presidency only and that it ought to be extended to the whole of India.

At the All India Depressed Classes Women's Conference held at Nagpur on 20th July, 1940, Dr. Ambedkar emphasised that there could not be any progress without women. He spoke, "I am a great believer in women's organization. I know what they can do to improve the condition of the society if they are convinced. In the eradication of social evils they have rendered great services".[2]

He underlined that women should learn to be clean and keep themselves away from all vices. They should educate their children and instil high ambition in them. The children's mind should be inculcated with the ideas that they are destined to be great. The sense of inferiority complex should be eliminated from their mind and heart.

After the adoption of the Constitution, Dr. Ambedkar was entrusted with a new responsibility of the Hindu Code Bill. He revised the Hindu Code prepared by the Rao's Committee and was darring enough to introduce the Hindu Code Bill on 5th February, 1951 in critical circumstances. The Hindu Code Bill introduced only four new items in the then existing law.

They were, abolition of the doctrine of the rights by birth, right to property to women, right to have share by daughters from the parent's property and provisions for divorce. Explaining the Bill, Dr. Ambedkar spoke that it would be wrong to describe the Hindu Code Bill as either radical or revolutionary. He said that the Bill, while according sanction to the new ways of progress, did not oppose the orthodox practices of progress. He further stated that the new Republican Constitution of India had given a positive direction that the Government should endeavour to prepare a civil code for the benefit of the country as a whole. The purpose of the Hindu Code Bill was to codify and modify certain provisions of the Hindu law. It was beneficial from the point of the country's oneness that the same set of laws should govern the Hindu social and religious life. The Hindu Code Bill was a right step towards a civil code.

On September 17th, 1951, a large demonstration of excited women took place around the Parliament House, when the long awaited Hindu Code Bill was supposed to be discussed and the police picketed all over to maintain law and order.[3] This truncated Bill was hotly discussed by the opponents. Suddenly, most of the members of the House got enraged on Dr. Ambedkar, because of his criticism on the story of Rama and Sita in his speech. There was much excitement and Nehru asked Dr. Ambedkar to drop the Bill. Describing Nehru's state of mind at this juncture one Journalist quoted Johnson's famous remark on Goldsmith—

"He wrote like an Angel and spoke like poor Paul" [4]

After that the Bill was let down in a tragic manner. And in the words of Dr. Ambedkar—

"It was killed and buried, unwept and unsung after four clauses were passed"

Dr. Ambedkar's disappointment was sore. He resigned his seat from the Cabinet on 27th September, 1951.[5]

Dr. Ambedkar in his resignation speech clarified, "The Hindu Code Bill was the greatest social reform measure undertaken by the Legislature in the country. No law passed by the Indian Legislature in the past or likely to be passed in the future, can be compared to it in point of its significance. To leave inequality between class and class, sex and sex, which is the soul of Hindu Society untouched and to go on passing legislation relating to economic problems is to make a farce of our Constitution and to build a palace on a dung heap".

Dr. Ambedkar was not at all convinced with the plea of the Prime Minister to abandon the Bill on the ground of the lack of time or that the opposition was strong. According to him, when the Bill was taken up in the party meeting, out of 120 only 20 were found against it. When the bill was taken in the party for discussion 44 Clauses were passed in about three and half hours time. This shows how much opposition there was against the Bill within the party. It was inevitable on the part of Nehru to think of the continuance of the Congress ascendancy in power and because of that he did not want to introduce such a drastic measure, which would have radicalised the Hindu Society. But, Dr. Ambedkar was keenly interested in the social reform, equal rights, for men and women and never thought of it from the political point of view. However, Nehru could not wholly be blamed for this debacle for which, many social, religious and political factors were responsible. He acted as a true politician under the prevailing situation of the time.

A few months before the incident, Justice Gajendragadkar of the Bombay High Court, a famous Jurist and Sanskrit Scholar in course of his speech on "Hindu Code Bill" before the students of the Karnataka University, had said—

> "If Dr. Ambedkar gives up Hindu Code, his achievement would go down in history as a piece of poetic justice indeed. Destiny, however, seemed unwilling to concede to the Law Minister of the full laurels of a modern Manu".

Dr. Ambedkar was excessively worried for the overgrowth of the population in India and he wanted certain measures should be introduced for the birth control. Viewing the contemporary situation he remarked—

> "The present keen struggle of life renders timely marriage impossible for many and they expose them to various diseases and habits. Many women become invalid for life and some even lose their lives by the birth of children in their diseased condition or in too rapid succession..Birth control is the only sovereign specific remedy that can do away with all these calamities. Wherever a woman is disinclined to bear a child for any reason whatsoever, she must be in a position to prevent conception and bringing forth progeny, which should be entirely dependent on the choice of women. Society would in no way profit by the addition of unwanted progeny".[6]

Dr. Ambedkar advised that everybody should marry after they become financially able. According to him, marriage was a liability. Keeping in mind the problem of population also, he advised that to have too many children was a crime. Parents must be responsible to give each child better start than they themselves had. The women should be on friendly terms with their husbands and if he does not agree it results into a slave relation between the husband and the wife.

The impassioned appeal to cast off evil practices and customs among certain sections of the depressed classes was made by Dr. Ambedkar at a meeting at the Damodar Thackersey Hall, Bombay in 1936. The meeting was largely attended by men and women belonging to the Devadasi, Patraje, Bhute, Aradhi and Jagiti communities, and was held to accord support to the mass conversion move inaugurated at Yeola. Dr. Ambedkar made a fervent appeal, especially to the women—

> "Whether you change your religion along with us or not, it does not matter much to me. But I insist that if you want to be with the rest of us, you must give up your disgraceful life. You must marry and settle down to a normal domestic life as women of other classes

> do. Don't continue to live under conditions, which inevitably drag you into prostitution".[7]

Dr. Ambedkar's impassioned love for the 'fallen' women as a whole community and his advice to rescue themselves from the despised and disgraceful life were quite meaningful. Dr.Ambedkar accorded equal status to women and men in every sphere and he also warned the women against the misuse of their rights. Therefore, it would be appropriate to regard Dr. Ambedkar as one of the saviours of Indian women. His contribution is unique and cherishable by the women of India. It should be the foremost duty of women's associations, groups and organisations to actively participate in the processes of social change and welfare. The women's movement needs to be strengthened to overcome the artificial divisions and boundaries created by geography, economy and ideology.

References

1. Vasant Moon (Ed), *Dr. Babasaheb Ambedkar : Writings and Speeches*, Vol. II, Government of Maharashtra, pp. 166-167.
2. B.Das (Ed), *Thus Spoke Ambedkar*, Vol.II, p. 195.
3. D. Keer, *Dr. Ambedkar : Life and Mission*, Bombay, 1961, p. 396.
4. *Ibid.*, p. 412.
5. *The Times of India*, 29th September, 1951.
6. Vasant Moon, op.cit., p. 264.
7. *The Times of India*, June 17, 1936, Vide Bhagwan Das (Ed) *Thus Spoke Ambedkar*, Vol. III, p. 195.

12

Socio-Economic Profile of the SCs : A Micro View in Hyderabad*

*J.S. Narayan Rao, Y. Pushpalatha***

This is a small sample study of the socio-economic conditions of SC population in Hyderabad, the capital of Andhra Pradesh, during 1991, from mostly slums, greatly inhabited by the SCs; in the birth centenary year of Dr. B.R.Ambedkar, a great son of India, as a token of our humble tribute.

We think that this is the first study of its kind, under-taken with the intention of knowing whether the SCs, following the constitutional guarantees and reservations,[1] and special programmes for their upliftment,[2] have made socio-economic progress in Independent India, which was the life-long ambition of Dr. Babasaheb and for which he expended his whole life.[3]

In what follows, we take a brief view of the SC population in the State.

SCs in Andhra Pradesh

The following tables give an evanescent view of the SC's in the State, in 1981, vis-a-vis the rest of the population. The 1991 picture has yet to come out.

* Thanks are due to our respendents. The paper is dedicated to them as a modest tribute to their dynamism, enterprise and hard-working nature.

** Member and Ph.D Scholar respectively, Department of Economics, Osmania University, Hyderabad 500 007.

TABLE 1
Profile of SCs in A.P.—1981

Sl. No.	Item	Size/Percentages
1.	State population	5.36 Crores
2.	SC population	0.796 Crores
3.	Percentage of SCs	15.2
4.	State Urbanisation (%)	23.3
5.	SC Urbanisation (%)	15.2
6.	State Literacy (%)	29.6
7.	SC Literacy (%)	17.64

Source: A.P. Statistical Abstract, Directorate of Economics and Statistics, Hyderabad.

Thus, the SCs fall behind the others in terms of both urbanisation and literacy,[4] by about 50 per cent. But SC urbanisation and literacy may be confined to mostly slums and some primary level of education or just 3 Rs. Still, urbanisation and literacy may afford some relief to our people from untouchability and poverty, urban anonymity and opportunity.

Andhra Pradesh accounts for about 8 percent of the total SC population of about 100 millions of India,[5] which is quite a formidable magnitude. Dr. Ambedkar would have called them his 'Nation' of great millions, or 1/6 of India. The State's SCs are greatly rural, and urbanisation, as said, can be expected to provide better socio-economic conditions to the SCs. Hyderabad stands unique in urbanisation as the 100 percent urban district of the State. It may set the tone or model for socio-economic upliftment of the SCs elsewhere in the State, as in Hyderabad the *dalits* are so near to the seat of power and Government, and the benefits meant for them may immediately come into their view as well as accrue to them also. They may be better provided with leadership, for Dr. Ambedkar was also, Bombay metropolitan based. From the city the message of Harijan upliftment may spread to the other parts of the State.

Demographically, where do our people stand in the city?

In the City

Hyderabad is the fifth largest metropolitan city of the country. It is a still fast expanding city, if the 1991 population of 4 million,[6] is an indication of it. However, just slums may be the abodes of our populace in the city, and they may also be confined to the periphery socio-economic sectors of the city. That is, they may belong almost exclusively to the "other" or the "second" city of slums and small living. The city is the home of, not only State administration, but also a number of industries, all of which may make the SCs to escape from their *drab* socio-economic conditions. A short demographic profile of the city with the place of the SCs in it is given in the following Table-2.

TABLE 2
A Profile of Hyderabad—1981

Sl. No.	*Items*	*Size and Percentage*
1.	Total population	22,60,702
2.	SC population	2,16,985
3.	Percentage of total	9.6
4.	Total literacy rate	56%
5.	SC literacy rate	NA

Source: Agrawal, *India: Economic Information, Year Book* 1990, National Publishing House, New Delhi, 1991, p. 76.

Thus, the SCs make about 10 percent population of the city, and they are found to be lagging behind the general populace in literacy. The city *dalit* population in time with the State average, 15 percent, needs to be raised to by 5 percent through migration.

The Sample

The study is based on a small sample of 120 households (HHs), varying in size from 2 to 15. In all, in the 120 HHs, there were 826 members. The sample, as such, is microscopic. Yet, it gives a good glimpse, though limited, of the socio-economic conditions of the metropolitan Harijans, which is worth viewing and interesting.

The sample localities and their sample sizes are given in the following table, as well as population sizes.

TABLE 3
Sample, Localities and Sizes

Sl.No.	Locality	Size of the HHs	Population/Members
1.	Chacha Nehru Colony	12	95
2.	Gandhinagar	12	50
3.	Poti Sri Ramulu Colony	12	75
4.	New Bhoiguda	12	80
5.	Ramaswami Compound	12	100
6.	Bansilalpet	12	120
7.	Addagutta	12	108
8.	Musheerabad	12	100
9.	Tilak Nagar	12	58
10.	Adikmet	12	40
	Total	120	826

The sample selection was 'random', in the sense of being chosen from across the city, from, its "four corners" from here and there. Same was the case with HHs selection. They are slum-samples. Non-slums *dalits* may have nothing to worry. Hence, our people are largely the 'second' city or slums people. They may be said to be 'second' class citizens but with others their inner-city migration may be encouraged.

Thus, the sample though microscopic, can be said to be well "Representative" scientific and competent enough to give a picture of the socio-economic conditions of the SCs.

In what follows, we present a brief socio-economic view of the population, commencing with untouchability and caste, which so much exercised Bharat Ratna Dr. B.R. Ambedkar, the prophet of our great billion.

Untouchability and Caste

Untouchability, during Ambedkar's time was the hallmark of our people. Nothing moved him greater than this. It is because of this, Babasaheb advocated conversion of his people to other religions, and at the fag end of his life, found solace in Buddhism by converting himself with a large mass of his followers to the Buddhist religion, on 14th October[7]

Vijayadashimi, 1956, at Nagpur. The great Babasaheb himself was a victim of the scourge, not only during his student days when he was made to sit apart and denied water from the school sources, but also as the Military Secretary of the Maharaja of Baroda, after his return from the Columbia University and the London School of Economics, when he was denied accommodation in Baroda and was not even handed over files by his upper-caste peons.[8] This makes an agonising reading. What of our people to day? Are they still untouchables[9] which is a 'crime' today?

Of course, untouchability is now an offence. Still, our sample do not appear to feel the pinch of it at all. They further told, all of them, with pride, that the upper-castes dare not practice untouchability. It was pleasing to find this once weak and oppressed community is quite independent and assertive today which makes one think that after-all the efforts of the Mahatma and Babasaheb in the *dalit* upliftment did not go waste.

They, moreover, have no bar whatsoever on temple entry. Thus, the twin problems stand annihilated. May be, the evils are still extant in the villages where the great mass of Harijan humanity dwells. The city and other urban areas may be immersed in their own problems, of inflation, unemployment and others to be bothered about untouchability. It is a non-issue in the city, to our great relief.

Far more, Dr. Ambedkar was in favour of inter-caste marriages and inter-dining. Three inter-caste marriages were reported in the sample, including both educated and uneducated. Thus, over a period of time, the caste barriers between the *dalits* and non-*dalits* may wholly crumble down and this must be regarded as one of the greatest happening of the Indian society, in contemporary times. Thus, our discovery of no untouchability should be regarded as a finding of great significance.

But, surprisingly, the community itself is not free from casteism. The three castes of the community in order of their social standing and numerical strengths are the following—

TABLE 4
Dalit Castes

S.No.	Caste	No. of Families	% to the total
1.	Mala Jangam	22	18.33
2.	Mala	26	21.66
3.	Madiga	72	60.00
	Total	120	100.00

Source: Primary Data.

Yet, the caste distinction were reported to be not rigid, there being free-mixing, inter-dining and inter-marriages, among the castes. It is also good that the Constitution does not recognise these castes. We do not know whether there are any marked differences in educational and economic attainment of the castes, nor is there any need to enquire into these differences. As all the three castes are greatly the dwellers of slums, there may not be marked difference and caste-conflict between the three.

The question untouchability having been greatly exercised, does still the SCs be called the SCs? Some thought, it appears, needs to be given to this. They may be brought into the category of BCs, something like the first of the BCs (A1), without of course any prejudice to their rights and protections. One wonders, as per our results, any Indian is a SC, socially. The raison-detre for classification of any Indians, untouchability, as SCs appears to be lost. This must be regarded as the greatest silent social revolution of our times and our contribution to indian culture 'new'.

Social Profile

This is given in tables 4-9, which pertain to family size, caste, education etc. of the SCs. Caste has already been exercised. *Supra*, that is 'Madiga' constitute the numerically superior caste, accounting for nearly 60 percent of the sample.

Next, what is the family size? Do our people, commonly accepted to be poor, over-breed and have large families? Is small family alien to them, explaining poverty? Table 5 provides some sort of answers to these queries/questions.

TABLE 5
Family Size

Sl.No.	Family Size	No. of Families	Percentage	Total Population	Percentage to the total
1.	2 - 5	50	41.66	198	24
2.	5 - 7	28	23.33	182	22
3.	7 - 10	26	21.66	230	28
4.	10 - 15	16	13.33	216	26.1
	Total	120	100.00	826	100.00

Source: Primary Data.

TABLE 6
Ages of the Family Heads

Sl.No.	Age group (Years)	M	F	Total	% to the Total
1.	20 - 30	34	—	34	28.33
2.	30 - 40	40	—	40	33.33
3.	40 - 50	16	10	26	21.66
4.	50 - 60	18	—	18	15.00
5.	60 -85	2	—	2	1.66
	Total	110	10	120	100.00

Source: Primary Data.

Vide Table-5, family sizes varied from two (man and woman) to 15, joint or extended families. Still the model size is 2-5 in which 50 families fall, constituting nearly 42 percent of the total 120 sample families. May be poverty makes people to stick together. In a study of ours,[10] pertaining to greatly BCs, the maximum family size was found to be 8. There is more 'socialism' of families in our people. However, large families even among our mutually sharing people appears to be a dying phenomenon, as only 16, or (13.33%) of the families fall in the largest family size of 10-15 members. Still, it cannot be denied that our people appear to breed or maintain larger families by Indian standards with 5 family sizes constituting about 60 percent of the total.

There is, of course, family planning but it does not start forthwith after 1 or 2, children as, say, in the upper castes children are not so un-welcome.

As per Table-6, youth appear to predominate in the affairs of the community and in running the HHs. 10 women, in 40-50 years, also join the sample, which may be regarded a novel feature of the community, which is according importance to women, though older, in family affairs.

However, the large families appear to have more earning members, as per, the following Table-7. Thus, ours is a labouring population.

TABLE 7
Earning Members

Sl.No.	*No. of Earners*	*No. of Families*	*% to the total*
1.	1	36	30.00
2.	2	42	35.00
3.	3	20	16.66
4.	4	14	11.66
5.	5	8	6.66
	Total	120	100.00

Source: Primary Data.

Thus, about 60 percent of the HHs have 5 members, and 66 percent of the families have more than 1 earning members. There are as many as 5 (five) earning members per family in some cases, though they are only 8 such families; thus, our population is working population where male, female and children too join in contributing to the family kitty. This, frankly, should be considered a great characteristics of the *dalit* people.

Education is also fairly wide-spread, vide Table-8, even with reference to the education of heads of the HHs. It comes to nearly 73 percent and extends from primary to medicine and engineering. The younger ones are more forwarding.

TABLE 8
Education

Sl.No.	*Education*	*No. of HHs*	*% to the Total*
1.	Illiterates	32	26.66

Sl.No.	Education	No. of HHs	% to the Total
2.	Primary	30	25.00
3.	Upper primary	16	13.33
4.	Secondary	30	25.00
5.	Intermediate	Nil	Nil
6.	Degree (B.A., B.Sc., B.Com.)	6	5.00
7.	Others like (Medicine, Engineering, M.Phil. etc.)	6	5.00
	Total	120	100.00

Source: Primary Data.

But the children should be 100 percent school going under the provision of free and compulsory education and many other incentives to the SC children[11], inspite of which, vide Table-9, 32 percent of the families are reported to be not sending their children to schools, mainly owing to poverty. So a special drive must be launched for 100 per cent schooling of the SC children and further incentives may be provided for the purpose. There may be another or many mini Ambedkars in making among these children. A fantastic thing observed about the school going children is that all of them were attending private schools and none was staying in hostels and none was in Telugu medium schools. So, our people are emerging into little elites, for good or bad. They cease to be *dalits* in this.

TABLE 9
Schooling of Children

Sl.No.	School going	Not going	Poverty	% to the Total
1.	88	—	—	74
2.	—	32	32	26
Total	88	32	32	100

Source: Primary Data.

Thus, the social picture that emerges of the people though not all rosy is also not much depressing, as might have been hypothesised. Mainly, illiteracy continue to plague the community. The levels of education of the community also, presently confined to primary (30), upper primary (16) and high school (30), need to be raised to above the secondary, and upto the secondary concentration may be made on technical and vocational education which may be presumed to be somewhat more bread-earning.

The social picture is singular in one respect, which is being completely free from the blemish of untouchability. Another, dowry appears not still a menacing problem. There appear to be no bride-burning cases. The stereotype picture of the SCs as untouchables, illiterate, over-breeding, cobblers, scavengers and other humble and *menial* servants holds no more in the Andhra metropolis. Good glad tidings on the centenary.

What of the economic picture?

Economic Picture

Far more important is the economic status of the community. The economic portrait is presented in Tables 10 to 18, succinctly.

First, the formal economic status of the community in terms of the "green" and "yellow" ration cards of Rs. 6000 and Rs. 6000, per family, per annum, which is presented in Table-10.

TABLE 10
Colour of the Cards

Sl.No.	*Items*	*Yellow*	*Green*	*Nil*	*Total*
1.	No. of cards	74	40	6	120
2.	% to the total	61.66	33.33	5	100

Source: Primary Data.

The "green" are the poor or people below the poverty line, and the "yellow" are non-poor. Then, as per this description, our community is greatly (61.66%) non-poor, and only (33.33%) are poor, who need to be specially provided for. Thus, surprisingly, poverty appears to be no special feature of the SCs in the city. Our paper, as such, is proving to be icnoclastic-breaking many socio-economic images of the *dalits*, particularly regarding untouchability and poverty. That, this is not a freak discovery is proved by Table-11 on monthly incomes.

TABLE 11
Monthly Income

(In Rs.)

S.No.	*Income Ranges*	*No. of Families*	*% to the Total*
1.	500 - 1000	24	20.00
2.	1000 - 2000	24	20.00
3.	2000 - 3000	28	23.33
4.	3000 - 4000	10	8.33
5.	4000 - 5000	18	15.00
6.	5000 - 6000	16	13.33
	Total	120	100.00

Source: Primary Data.

TABLE 12
Expenditure

Sl.No.	*Expenditure Ranges*	*Number of Families*	*% to the Total*
1.	200 - 500	16	13.33
2.	500 - 1000	18	15.00
3.	1000 - 2000	28	23.33
4.	2000 - 3000	36	30.00
5.	3000 - 4000	10	8.33
6.	4000 - 5000	10	8.33
7.	5000 - 6000	2	1.66
	Total	120	100.00

Source: Primary Data.

In fact, according to Table-11, as there is no HH below Rs. 500 per month, the poverty line population further comes down from 33 percent or so of the green ration cards. What is more, not only their incomes are not less than Rs. 500 but also go upto a fantastic Rs. 10,000. A good number of families, 52 (43.33%), have incomes between Rs. 1000 to Rs. 3000. One thing more, the families, almost all of them, appear to deal in five digits or even six digits viz., thousands of rupees per month regarding, income, expenditure, saving, as well as debt, as obvious from the following tables on expenditure, savings, debt and housing, etc.

Hope, we are not sending wrong signals regarding the community, which emerges as a hard working and enterprising community. The community needs to be helped in coming out from slums to the other city or the first city. Yet, it is a tribute to the enterprise of the community that even in drab slum environment, they are trying to enliven their lives. They appear to be lending dignity to the slums.

TABLE 13
Savings

Sl.No.	*Item*	*Banks*	*Chits*	*Gold*	*Private*
1.	Savings Families	66	70	28	Nil
2.	Percentage to Total	55	58.4	23.33	Nil
3.	Non-Saving Families	54	50	92	Nil
4.	Percentage to Total	45	41.60	76.66	Nil

Source: Primary Data.

TABLE 14
Debt

Sl.No.	*Debt Ranges Rs.*	*No. of Families*	*% to the Total*
1.	No debt	42	35.00
2.	5000 - 10000	38	31.66
3.	10000 - 20000	18	15.00
4.	20000 - 30000	10	8.33
5.	30000 - 50000	8	6.66
6.	50000 - 200000	4	3.33
	Total	120	100.00

Source: Primary Data.

TABLE 15
Causes and Agencies of Debt

Sl.No.	*Causes*	*No. of Families*	*% to the Total*	*Govt.*	*Non-Govt.*
1.	Marriages	36	30	18	28
2.	House construction	18	15	16	2
3.	Family maintenance	16	13.33	10	-

Sl.No.	*Causes*	*No. of Families*	*% to the Total*	*Govt.*	*Non-Govt.*
4.	Business	8	6.66	4	-
	Total	78	65	48	30

Source: Primary Data.

TABLE 16

Housing

(in Rs.)

Sl.No.	No. of Rooms	*No. of Families*	*Percentage*	*Value Ranges*	*No. of Own*	*Families Rented*	*% to Col. 6*	*% to Col. 7*
1	*2*	*3*	*4*	*5*	*6*	*7*	*8*	*9*
1.	1	16	13.33	10-20	26	26	21.66	21.66
2.	2	28	23.33	20-30	16	-	13.33	-
3.	3	36	30.00	30-50	30		25.00	
4.	4	26	21.66	50-100	10		8.33	
5.	5	6	5.00	100-200	8		6.66	
6.	6	4	3.33	200-500	4		3.33	
7.	7	2	1.66		94	26	78.33	21.66
8.	10	2	1.66					
		120	100.00	Grand total	94+26 = 120		78.33+21.66 = 100	

Source: Primary Data.

TABLE 17

Housing Facilities

Sl.No.	*Having/ Not Having*	*W*	*WC*	*P*	*BR*	*K*
1.	Having	64	92	120	80	60
2.	Percentage	53	76.7	100	66.66	50
3.	Not having	56	28	—	40	60
4.	Percentage	46.66	23.7	—	33.33	50

Source: Primary Data.

TABLE 18
Consumer Durables

Sl.No.	*Items*	*No. of Families*	*% to the Total*
1.	Fan	90	75
2.	Cycle	90	75
3.	TV - BW/CT	80	66.66
4.	Scooter	48	40
5.	Gas	30	25
6.	Fridge	10	8.33

Source: Primary Data.

Monthly expenditure which is a better index to the state of economic being of a people, ranges from Rs. 200 - Rs. 6,000 per month (Table 12). At the most, Rs. 200 - Rs. 500 expenditure group may be said to be living in poverty or want of adequate quantity of food, and other minimum needs of life. But these are only 16 families or 13.33 percent of the sample. Most of the families, 64 (53.33%) are in the expenditure group of Rs. 1000 - Rs. 3000, 22 families are in the Rs. 3000 - Rs. 6000 expenditure group. It must strike one that the low expenditure ranges, Rs. 200-Rs. 6000, then the income ranges Rs. 500 - Rs. 10000, give out a parsimonious community which is good for the economy and good for the families in the present state of Indian economic development, marked by a stagnant saving rate (S/Y), at some 22 percent[12]

That our community is very economical or parsimonious is evident from the saving data also (Table 13). As many as 70 families are found indulging in savings, in cash and kind viz., gold. The cash savings are in banks and chit funds. It comes as a surprise that the chits are more popular than banks. The lure of "yellow" metal gold is also there in some 30 families. Thus, they are well-managing their savings among banks, chits and gold. No land-savings were reported. Meaning, people are not speculative.

The community also appears to play with great amounts of debt-(Table 14) of Rs. 5000 - Rs. 2 lakhs. 42 families were debt-free. The most common debt range is Rs. 5000 - 10000 in which 38 families borrowed, 28 from private sources and 18 from government. The rest of the borrowing groups are from government which is a greatly redeeming feature of the debt.

And coming to the causes of debt (Table 15), marriages are the most important factor putting 36 families in debt. The other factors are housing, consumption and business. Thankfully, only 16 families borrowed for consumption. An unfortunate feature of private borrowings is the heavy rates of interest varying 5 to 10 percent which may be putting the families in 'debt trap', some 28 families may be in this trap before they be released.

Coming to housing (Table 16) which is very crucial in urban areas, particularly in metropolitan city like Hyderabad, 94 families were having their own houses, ranging in value from Rs. 10000 - Rs. 5 lakhs, and rooms from 1 to 10. Those who were living in rented 'houses' were having not more than 2 rooms, and paying rent of Rs. 50 - Rs. 200 per month, making housing an important constraint of the people, some dwelt 'free' in garages.

Regarding housing facilities like water, power, bath rooms, kitchen, lavatory etc., water appears to be the most important facility lacking in about 56 families who have to depend on public water taps, regarding which surprisingly there were no complaints, giving out no 'complaining' people.

Taking consumer durables, 75 percent each possessed fans and cycles, 66.67 percent TVs, mostly portable B.W., and 40 percent scooters and 25 percent gas. It was found that firewood has disappeared completely as a medium of cooking, marking the cooking medium advancement of our people from firewood and coal to kerosene and gas, no small advancement.

Thus, the socio-economic picture of the Hyderabad *dalits* is none to unhappy and it is a good deal to the efforts of Dr. Ambedkar, who is a household name among the people, along with the Mahatma, whether one likes it or not.

It does not mean that all is well with the city SC population. They are greatly slum dwellers, and whatever "prosperity" they possess must be attributed to their labouring characteristics. Even if they cannot be taken out from the slums for the time being, slum improvement programmes can be undertaken, in the SC slums, first, with the provision of enough social infrastructure like schools, training centres, child care centres and so on. It was observed that none of the *"bastis"* possessed any training centres, night schools, adult education, community centres, libraries, reading rooms and dispensaries, playing facilities, and so on. Why? Our people should 'demand' them.

They also complained about poor housing facilities. The important problem is 2 kg rice scheme under which 25kg per family a month ration was stated to be insufficient and wanted it to be raised to 50 kgs atleast, with the supply of a good quality rice.

Surprisingly, our people were a contended lot, not a complaining and grumbling type, which must be acknowledged as a great quality of the people with thousands of years of history of suffering and injustice. But, they are "awakened" people who can no more be taken for granted.

Another, all the yellow card holder wanted to be considered for green cards. But, unfortunately, the people were not inclined towards self-employment. The educated youth complained of discrimination and corruption in the self-employment training programmes which calls for special training programmes for the SCs under voluntary agencies as the ISRA.* Further, these SC schemes also need to be evaluated by the voluntary bodies, to see that they derive benefits from the schemes.

References

1. *Articles*
   15, Prohibition of discrimination on grounds of religion, race, caste, sex, or place of birth.
   17, Abolition of untouchability.
   46, Promotion of educational and economic interests of SC and ST and other weaker sections.
   330, Reservation of seats for SCs and STs of the People.
   332, Reservations of seats for SCs and STs in the Legislative Assemblies.
   335, Claims of SC and ST to Services and Posts.
   338, Special Officer for SCs, STs etc.
   Vide: COI, *The Consititution of India*. Manager of Government of India Press, New Delhi, 1949; Verma, G.P., *Caste Reservations in India, Change Publications, Allahabad, 1980, p 146; V.P. Bharatiya, Religion State Relationship and Constitutional Rights in India,* Deep and Deep Publications, New Delhi, 1987, p. 153.
2. *The Schemes*

---

* The senior author is Secretary of the body, devoted to the SCs and STs and other Weaker Sections.

The schemes include: Hostels (2300), Residential Schools (63), Scholarships, Training Programmes (Rs. 1 crore), Housing Plots, Housing Distribution of Land, SC Financial Corporation; Special Component plans which spend 15 per cent of plan funds on the SCs, and SC welfare schemes which aggregated to Rs. 200 crores, in 1990-91.
Vide: Andhra Pradesh Darshini, Visalandhra Publications, Hyderabad, 1987, pp 1083-84, Prasant, *Social Engineering and Constitutional Protection of Weaker Sections in India*, Deep and Deep Publications, New Delhi, 1980, p. 35; Pantine, K., *Caste in Contemporary India, Beyond Organic Solidarity*, Rawal Publications, Jaipur 1984, p. 40; Uma Ramaswamy, "Education and Inequality", *Economic and Political Weekly*, Vol. XX, No. 36, Sept. 7, 1985, p. 1523.

3. Barathi, K.S., *Foundation of Ambedkar Thought*, Daltsons Publications, Nagpur, 1990, p. 64; Manmohan Singh, "Ambedkar: The Relentless Crusader", *Yojana*, Vol. 35, No. 36, April 15, 1991, pp. 10-11; Shakunthala Dhawan, "Dr. B.R.Ambedkar; Apostle of Social Justice", *Yojana*, Vol. 35, No. 6, April 1991, pp. 12- 14.
4. Victor, S.D'Sowza, *Development Planning and Structural Inequalities*, Sage Publications, New Delhi, 1990, p. 74.
5. *A.P. Statistical Abstract, Directorate of Economics and Statistics*, Hyderabad, 1983, p. 43.
6. *Deccan Chronicle*, 25 March, 1991, p. 1.
7. Narendra Jadhav, "Neglected Economic Thought and Babasaheb Ambedkar", *Economic and Political Weekly*, Vol. XXVI, No. 15, 13th April, 1991, pp. 980 to 982.
8. *Ibid.*, p 986.
9. As per Article 17; *op. cit.*
10. Rao, Narayan, J.S. and Y. Pushpalatha, "Socio-Economic Conditions and Hotel Workers in Hyderabad-Secunderabad", *Vartha*, Special Number on Informal Sector Labour, 1991 (forthcoming).
11. Murthy, S.K., *Contemporary Problems and Current Trends in Education*, Prakash Brothers, Ludhiana, 1988, p. 98.
12. Roy, Thithankar, Kunalsen, "Changes in Saving Rate and its Implications for Growth", *Economic and Political Weekly*, Vol. XXVI No. 26, April 20, 1991, pp. 1055 to 1058; Roy Choudhuri, Gnanand Bagchi (Eds) (1990), *Domestic Savings in India*, NIPFP, Vikas Publications, New Delhi.

13

Dr. B.R. Ambedkar - A Boon For The Industrial Labour*

*B.N.Vinod Rao***

In every country large scale industrialisation has adversely affected the working class people due to long working hours, industrial fatigue, bad environmental conditions at the place of work, industrial hazards, concentration of population in dirty slums, insanitation and industrial diseases etc. But, in our country, Dr. Ambedkar felt as his duty to do as much as possible, to improve the conditions of the industrial labour who were hit hard as a result of industrialisation.

Dr. Ambedkar was the Chief Architect of our Constitution and the leader of depressed classes. He has been stamped as a Pro-British and parochial caste leader. But very few have studied him as a traveller of thought and as a patriot with ultimate loyality to his mother-land.[1]

Keeping the welfare of poor, depressed especially workers, in August, 1936, Dr. Ambedkar founded a new political party called "The Independent Labour Party" and drew up comprehensive programme which answered all the immediate needs and grievances of the landless, poor tenants, agriculturists and industrial workers.

The party believed that the fragmentation of holdings and the pressure of population over them were the causes of the poverty of the agriculturists and the way out was rehabilitation of old industries and starting new ones. In order to raise the efficiency and productive capacity of the workers, the party de-

---

* The author wishes to thank Prof. J.S. Narayan Rao. Faculty Member, Department of Economics, Osmania University, Hyderabad for his encouragement in preparing and improving this paper.

** Lecturer in Economics Govt. College, Malakpet, Hyderabad-36.

clared itself in favour of an extensive programme of technical education and the principle of State management and State ownership of industries where necessary. The manifesto promised to undertake legislation to protect agricultural tenants from the exactions and evictions by the landlords and to extend the same benefits to them as would be provided for industrial workers, with suitable changes. For the benefit of industrial workers the party would endeavour to introduce legislation to control the employment, dismissal and promotion of employees in factories, to fix maximum hours of work, to make provision for adequate wages and for leave with pay and to provide cheap and sanitary dwellings for workers. Unemployment, it observed, would be relieved by starting public works.[2]

Dr. Ambedkar joined as a member in "Viceroy Labour Executive Council" on July 20th, 1942 and played a vital role in amending the Industrial Acts and achieved benefits like reduction of working hours, leave with pay, maternity leave, legislation relating to factories and mines, social security, welfare outside of the work, the Employees Provident Fund and Miscellaneous Provisions Act, Stopping Retrenchment and Compensation Act. He argued that labour legislation was essentially a socio-economic legislation pertaining to various human problems in relation to Industry.

In the past, there were no harmonious relations between labour and management due to lack of understanding. Like in Capitalistic Economics, in India also Ambedkar observed exploitation of labour, to avoid exploitation, Ambedkar advised—

1. the industries which are key industries or which may be declared to be key industries shall be owned and run by the State; and
2. the industries which are not key industries but which are basic industries shall be owned by the State and shall be run by the State or Corporations established by the State.[3]

Dr. Ambedkar introduced a Tripartite Committee to improve the labour conditions like wages, bonus, leave with wages, and host of other matters to prevent and settlement of disputes between employees and employers. The Committee consists of three members which represents Government, Employees and

Employers to solve their problems through discussions. The aim of the Tripartite Committee was to bring the parties to industrial disputes "together for mutual settlement of differences in a spirit of cooperation and good will".[4]

Under the Chairmanship of Dr. Ambedkar, the first Labour Conference was held on 7.8.1942, when representatives of employers and workers were also invited to take part in that conference. In his address Dr. Ambedkar said—

"It is for the first time in the history of these labour conferences that the representatives of the employers and employees have been brought face to face within the ambit of a joint conference."[5]

He discussed in labour conferences and covered several aspects like wage differences, labour welfare funds, industrial dispute and preventive Acts, etc. He conducted the Labour Conference four times and suggested several measures for the labour welfare to the Government and also made the Government to implement those suggestions.

Government of India passed Mines Act for the welfare of labour who worked in the coal mines on 31-1-1944 and Labour Welfare Fund was established. The main source of the welfare fund was 25 NP tax per tonn levied on the coal brought out from coal mines. As the fund was very little the Government failed to take steps for the welfare of labour. In this connection Dr. Ambedkar played a vital role in increasing the labour welfare fund by doubling levying of tax on the coal brought out. The labour welfare fund was increased and utilised for the safeguarding of the health and safety of the workers. It also took care of drinking water for workers, facility of education, cultural activities etc., which had promoted their welfare.

On 8.4.1946 Dr. Ambedkar introduced a resolution in Central Assembly and an Act was passed for the welfare of labour of Mica Mines. The Act provided several amenities to child and woman labour like working conditions, working hours and wage differences etc. Later the Act was very helpful to various Mica Mines Labour Welfare Organizations in India.

Later being a member of Viceroy Committee he took several steps to amend the Mica Mines Act by 2 times. Due to amendments several amenities were extended to the women labour of

Mica Mines like arrangement of cradles for infants and appointment of maids for nursing their children etc.

Dr. Ambedkar tried to help not only the industrial labour women, but also the other women. He said that it should be the foremost duty of Indian women to integrate themselves to help their fellow-sisters, who are under the despised and degraded professions like the flesh-trade, beggary etc. So educated women should join social work to educate, organise and unite all depressed women.[6]

During his tenure Dr. Ambedkar took steps to amend the Maternity Benefits Act and the Workmen Compensation Act of 1923. After the amendments, the compensation to the workers who die during work was increased from Rs. 4,000 to Rs. 4,500 and to the workers who were fully handicapped, the compensation was increased from Rs. 5,600 to Rs. 6,300. According to the Maternity Benefits Act, several amenities were provided to women labour working inside as well as outside the Mica Mines.

In 1944, Dr. Ambedkar initiated to amend the Industrial Act of 1934 with several modifications. According to the modifications, washing facilities were arranged to the labour in every industry and changes also took place in working hours and earned leave facilities. It also followed the pattern of England in working hours i.e., 48 hours work per week in India, 10 days earned leave for adults and 14 days earned leave for child labour. Apart from this Dr. Ambedkar recommended more holidays and less working hours to the labour during war time.

Whenever there was dispute between workers and employers due to misunderstanding, it lead to mental agony also. In this connection to avoid the problem Dr. Ambedkar has introduced Industrial Workers Act which does not bring any pressure in working hours and productive efficiency.

Dr. Ambedkar noted that capitalistic economy debases noble feelings of workers. Therefore, Ambedkar pleaded for its early destruction from the world. Capitalism breeds exploitive values and therefore it must be abolished and be replaced by the establishment of genuine socialism[7]. Ambedkar's concept of Constitutional State Socialism is unique and more humanistic because he believed that democratic organisation must remain its concomitant part for otherwise the abolition of capitalism would necessarily lead to dictatorship wherein democracy might not be possible and dignity of labour be underrated.

As Dr. Ambedkar understood the need and role of Trade Unions for labour welfare, he introduced a Bill in Central Assembly on 8.11.1943 for the recognisation of Trade Unions and the following three principles were initiated in the Act. They are—

1. The management should give recognisation to the Trade Union;
2. The management should lay some conditions to recognise the Trade Unions; and
3. If any management fails to recognise their Trade Unions it may be treated as violation of the Act and also considered as an offence.

On 11.4.1946, Dr. Ambedkar had introduced a Bill to frame advisory boards consisting of the representatives of labour and management for pay revision of labour.

For determination of minimum wages to labour and their welfare Dr. Ambedkar had initiated to appoint several committee like Provincial Committee, Enquiry Committee and Labour Investigation Committee, etc.

As already mentioned Dr. B.R. Ambedkar became the labour member of the Viceroy Executive Council on July 20, 1942, but resigned in the third week of June, 1946. He was thus in office only for about four years. The period, though short, is nevertheless a watershed, if not a landmark, in the history of labour legislation and labour welfare in this country.[8]

Dr. Ambedkar helped a lot not only for the upliftment of *dalits* but also the labourers through amendments of several enactments and legislations in Central Assembly. So the Industrial Labour Community of our country should be ever grateful to Dr. Ambedkar who rendered his selfless services. So we can say that Dr. Ambedkar is a boon for the Indian Industrial Labour.

References

1. Kelkar, B.K., "Dr. B.R. Ambedkar - The Nationalist Thinker", *Organiser,* 13th April, 1986.

2. Keer, Dhananjay, *Dr. Ambedkar : Life and Mission*, Popular Prakashan, Bombay, 1991, pp. 285-286.
3. Ambedkar, B.R., *State Socialism*, Bheem Patrika Publications, Jalandhar, 1990, p.10.
4. Bhagolival, T.N., *Economics of Labour and Industrial Relations*, Sahitya Bhavan, Agra, 1981, p. 353.
5. Baisantry, D.K., *Dr. Ambedkar-A Pioneer of Labour Welfare*, Buddhist Publishing House, Jalandar, 1990, pp. 5-6.
6. Mallik, Basant Kumar, "Ambedkar on Women's Progress", *Mainstream*, April, 1987.
7. Singh, Gian, *Dr. Ambedkar and Humanism*, Bheem Patrika Publications, Jalandhar, 1990, p.14.
8. Baisantry, D.K., *op. cit.*, p.5.

14

Quality of Life of Scheduled Castes—Facts and Issues

*Dr. A. Somasekhar**

Social Development has emerged as dominant paradigm in the third world with growing concern to have a match between quantitative economic growth and qualitative improvement in life issues in order to raise people from their poverty (Marsen-D, 1989). Development now a days cannot be treated merely as an expansion of income and wealth but as a process of enlarging peoples capabilities. Physical quality of life index has become the order of the day for Policy makers and Planners to raise the levels of living of weaker sections through appropriate policies and programmes.

Dr. Ambedkar's social philosophy, his thoughts and ideas and sermons are very much relevant to present times. Prior to Independence, in one of his speeches he stated that the salvation lies in higher education, higher employment and better ways of earning a living. His relentless fight for social equality, abolition of untouchability and annihilation of casteism inspired the State and Central Governments to enact suitable legislations. He gave the clarion call to the Nation on January, 26, 1950, "we have equality in politics and inequality in social and economic life. We must remove this contradiction at the earliest moment or else those who suffer from inequality will blow up the structure of political democracy". Dr. Ambedkar's speeches and sermons

---

* Director, Scheduled Castes Research and Training Institute, Telugu Samkshema Bhavan, Masab Tank, Hyderabad.

can be the basis for the development of all social groups in the country.

In the social structure of our country, 1/5th of the population suffers from social and economic handicaps and disabilities and these underprivileged groups are the SCs, STs and other weaker sections. These groups lack adequate opportunities for self-development, especially in increasing their income and employment. In Andhra Pradesh, there are 33 ST, 59 SC and 93 backward class communities constituting 58% of the total population. The social, economic and cultural conditions vary among these groups. The common problems of the weaker sections are acute poverty, social discrimination, illiteracy and exploitation. The Scheduled Castes of Andhra Pradesh are spread over all the districts of the State and they are at various levels of socio-economic development. They still suffer from social disabilities and occupationally they are linked with impure occupations. Many schemes have been introduced to improve the living conditions of the people especially in rural areas during planning era with different approaches and strategies which laid emphasis on the upliftment of disadvantaged sections of the society.

Welfare Programmes

Approaches and strategies have been changing from plan to plan for improving the living standards of population and eradication of poverty. Though exploitation which is a result of economic backwardness has been recognised as a major problem for the development of SCs long back, however, focus was more on extending educational and social amenities to SCs. This situation might be due to more concentration of planning authorities on the concept of "Welfare" rather than "Development". The planning experience reveals that a more realistic view was taken from IV Five Year Plan onwards about the relationship between "growth", "distribution" and "social justice" by implementing the schemes like GDA, SFDA, MFAL, IRDP, DRDA, ITDA, etc., which are specially aimed for "an assault on rural poverty". During IV Five Year Plan, new programmes like Housing Federation for SCs and STs were introduced. However, by the end of IV Five Year Plan, it was evident that the strategies for the development of these disadvantaged groups would have to be based on comprehensive development especially economic resource development, so that these sections of the population would acquire the ability to utilize the fruits of general economic development arising from various sectoral development programmes. From V Five Year Plan onwards, more emphasis has been laid on economic development of SCs since it is found to be a necessary pre-condition to their social development. The Working Group Report for development of SCs VI Plan rightly pointed out, "Notwithstanding this extremely adverse situation, the SCs contribute significantly to the sustenance and growth of the production systems of the country and the nation's economy, rarely has any section of a nation contributed so much for so long in return for so little. Indian society owes the SCs a heavy moral and material debt, yet to be discharged".

The Special Component Plan for SCs has also been formulated and detailed into regular 5 year plans from VI Five Year Plan. Integrated Rural Development Programme as an approach to rural development has been adopted for improving the conditions of the poor by reducing poverty and improving the quality of life in the rural areas. The VII Five Year Plan in A.P. has set out an important objective of "better balance in levels of economic and social development through appropriate policies for the development of irrigation, power, industries and social services in drought affected and other backward/tribal areas."[1]

Plan Outlays

There has been a rapid increase in the budget provision for the welfare of Scheduled Castes and for social security measures during the last one decade. The budget of the Social Welfare Department was Rs. 78.57 crores for the year 1982-83 which was increased to Rs. 240.82 crores during 1991-92. Though the increase in budget appears to be high in absolute terms the increase might be nullified due to inflation.

The Social Welfare Department is mainly responsible for planning, monitoring and execution of several programmes under Human Resource Development (Education and Training), Economic Betterment Schemes, Health and Housing and Social Security measures. The schemes which have been under implementation are maintenance of hostels and children homes, sanction of various types of scholarships, supply of nationalised text books, training programmes, land acquisition for house sites, rehabilitation of bonded labourers, provision of civic amenities in SC localities, coordination of work relating to social security schemes, implementation of protection of Civil Rights Act., etc.

During the planning era, the State Government provided separate financial allocations and formulated socio-economic programmes to improve the lot of SCs. The following table shows the plan-wise outlays for the socio-economic development of SCs.

TABLE 1
Plan-wise Outlays for Scheduled Castes - A.P.[2]

Plan Period	*State Plan Outlay*	*Outlay on Programmes of SCs*	*Percentage of Allocation on SCs*
First Plan (1951-56)	94.98	1.30	1.37
Second Plan (1956-61)	188.60	1.53	0.81
Third Plan (1961-66)	312.66	1.72	0.55
Annual Plan			
1966-67	93.39	0.11	0.11
1967-68	63.01	0.08	0.14
1968-69	74.36	0.09	0.13
Fourth Plan (1969-75)	444.19	2.33	0.52
Fifth Plan (1975-80)	1039.93	7.14	0.69
Sixth Plan (1980-85)	3100.00	110.00	3.55
Seventh Plan (1985-90)	7500.00	214.00	2.85

Sovrce : Hand Book of Social Welfare Statistics, Social Welfare Department, Government of Andhra Pradesh, Hyderabad, 1990.

The percentage of outlay on Scheduled Castes to total outlay has been on decreasing trend upto IV Five Year Plan. IncreaseIInd PROOF in percentage of outlay has been noticed from IV Plan onwards.

Education

Emphasis has been laid on provision of educational facilities to SCs, in terms of sanction of pre-matric and post-matric scholarships, establishment of hostels, free supply of books, slates and clothes and exemption from fees upto the end of III Five Year Plan. Several new programmes such as institution of merit scholarships for high school students during IV Five Year Plan and large number of pre-matric scholarships for the children of scavengers and book banks in medical and engineering colleges were introduced during V Five Year Plan. In order to impart quality education to SCs, more than half of the Department budget (51.87%) is spent on education. The achievements in the field of education for Scheduled Castes are briefly given below—

1.	S.W. Residential Schools	68
2.	Strength in S.W Residential Schools	23,000
3.	Ashram Schools for SC Children	8
4.	No. of students in Ashram Schools	480
5.	SC students admitted in Public Schools and best available schools	920
6.	Model Residential I.T.Is.	4
7.	Model Residential Polytechnics	3
8.	Residential Jr. Colleges	3
9.	No. of Government Hostels	2,257
10.	Boarders in Hostels	2,31,090
11.	Student managed hostels	440
12.	Strength in student managed hostels	1,01,491
13.	College attached hostels	199
14.	Strength in College attached hostels	13,790
15.	Special hostels for improving results of boarders in Xth Class	133
16.	No. of Vimukthi Hostels	108
17.	Construction of Hostel Buildings	1,007
18.	Construction of Residential School Buildings	
19.	Pre-matric scholarships—No. of students	6,90,000
20.	Scholarships for 1st and 2nd classes	5,00,000
21.	Stipends in ITIs	2,605
22.	Post-matric Scholarships	1,37,000
23.	Research Scholarships	594

Several facilities such as food, accommodation, dresses, text books, note books, cosmetics, bedding material, plates and glasses, trunk boxes, tuition, medical facilities, games material etc., are provided free of cost in hostels for improving the quality of life of boarders. Further book banks in colleges and professional colleges and supply of essential text books for SCs students in Engineering and Medical Colleges and supply of books and instruments in Polytechnics and ITIs have been under implementation. Due to provision of several facilities for SC students, the percentage of result have shown remarkable increase especially in Social Welfare Residential Schools (77%) when compared to general schools in the State (48%) during the year 1991. The new scheme of special hostels which was introduced during 1990-91 by pooling 9th and 10th classes boarders of the existing Social Welfare Hostels has also shown improvement in 10th class results from (% Year) to (% Year).

Training

Training to SC candidates is essential to improve the human resources in terms of skill endowments, awareness, knowledge and competitive spirit. Different types of training programmes have been taken up in various trades like dress-making, typewriting, shorthand, motor driving etc., besides coaching programmes for Civil Services, Staff recruitment examinations, entrance examinations like EAMCET, ECET, CEEP etc.

The achievements under the scheme of training programmes are as follows—

1.	No. of SC candidates finally selected for I.A.S., I.P.S., and Allied Services from A.P. Study Circle-1980-1990.	..	68
2.	No. of SCcandidates admitted in professional courses from PETCs during 1984 - 85 to 1990-91 (excluding) Tirupati	..	
3.	Training of SCAdvocates in Administration of Justice (1982-83 to 1990-91)	..	
4.	No. of SC candidates trained in 27 Vocational Training Centres and 18 garment production centres.	..	600+320

Economic Betterment Schemes

The APSCCFC has been implementing economic betterment schemes with emphasis on Agriculture, Horticulture, Irrigation etc., Irrigation master plan was prepared with an estimated outlay of Rs. 679,02 crores to irrigate 5,22,109 acre of land and benefit 3,59,569 SC families. Horticulture Plan with a total outlay of Rs.33.00 crores was prepared with a loan assistance of Rs. 18.23 crores from National SC & ST Development Corporation.

A programme to purchase agricultural land to landless SC candidates is under implementation to benefit 5,700 SC candidates with a total allocation of Rs. 573.00 lakhs. Government have assigned land under land ceiling and waste lands to SC people to an extent of about 12.00 lakhs so far. Various economic development schemes such as development of surplus land, provision of irrigation facilities, horticulture, sericulture, poultry, shopping complexes etc. have been under implementation by APSCCFC since inception with a total outlay of Rs. 763.45 crores from (1974-75 to 1990-91) covering 21.32 lakh SC families.

Civic Amenities and House Sites

The Housing Corporation for SCs and STs was established during IV Five Year Plan period to look after the housing needs. In order to improve the quality of life of SCs Government have been providing civic amenities like internal roads, path-ways and approach roads to SC localities and providing drinking water facilities. Besides these, Vimukthi Programme is also under implementation in all Municipalities. A massive programme of acquisition of land for providing house sites to SCs at free of cost has been taken up benefiting 26,75,781 beneficiaries to the extent of 1,56,926 acres of house sites. Besides acquisition of house sites, construction of houses numbering was also taken up under Weaker Section Housing Programme.

Social Security and Other Welfare Measures

The Social Security and other schemes have been introduced from V Five Year Plan. The social security schemes comprise maintenance of children homes for orphans, social security pensions to the old indigent people, poor widows and landless agricultural labourers, insurance scheme to rickshaw pullers and rehabilitation of bonded labour and Jogin women. Altogether 35,810 bonded labourers were identified and 25,737 rehabilitated besides identification of 16,267 Jogin women. The schemes like house sites, admission of children into schools and hostels, and assignment, land development, digging of wells etc., are taken up under rehabilitation of Jogin women especially in Nizamabad, Karimnagar, and Kurnool districts. The old age pensions to benefit 2,29,000 pensioners and widow pensions to 52,405 beneficiaries and 564,000 pensions to landless agricultural workers were taken up to provide minimum security of life for them.

Special Cells were created to look after the implementation of PCR Act, reservations and facilities for SCs in various sectors especially education and protection from exploitation. A.P. is the first State in the country in setting up mobile courts in all the districts to deal with the case of atrocities and crimes against SCs. Top most priority is being given to ensure prompt action against offenders indulged in atrocities on SCs. The District Collectors and SP's are made responsible for strict enforcement of the Protection of Civil Rights Act, 1955 in the district. Under the new Act of prevention of atrocities, there is a provision for special courts which should be sessions courts. Three sessions courts in Guntur, Mahaboob Nagar and Chittor districts have been sanctioned during the current year.

Quality of Life

The land reforms measures such as abolition of intermediary tenures, confirmation of ownership rights to tenants, imposition of land ceilings, distribution of surplus lands, land assignment etc., besides providing a productive assets base for a large number of rural landless poor especially SCs have also removed to a considerable extent the institutional and motivational obstacles for modernisation of agriculture and establishment of a more egalitarian social structure. The land assignment to different social groups from 1-11-1969 to 31-12-1990 indicate that 37,07,476.39 acres have been assigned of which 11.17 lakh acres have been assigned to SCs (30.1) in the State.

Inspite of various achievements and policy initiatives the poverty remains to be the basic problem especially among the disadvantaged sections of the society. The 42 round of NSSD

(1986-87) reveal that 47.57 and 41.85 percent of persons and house holds respectively are below poverty line in rural areas of our State.

The social, cultural and economic gap between the SCs and general population is indicated below—

TABLE 2
Levels of Development

Sl..No		*SCs*	*General Population*
1.	Compound growth rate of population	3.33	2.10
2.	Percentage of urban population to total population	15.19	23.32
3.	Percentage of literacy	17.65	29.94
4.	Work participation rate	54.30	42.30
5.	Percentage of workers engaged in Agricultural Sector (Agrl. Lab. & Cultivators)	86.50	71.90
6.	Percentage of non-workers to total population	12.53	54.24
7.	Percentage of workers engaged in non-agricultural sectors	13.50	28.10
8.	Percentage of irrigated area to net area sown	21.00	38.95
9.	Average size of holding (Hect)	0.95	1.72
10.	Percentage of Harijanwads/villages electrified	92.00	98.50
11.	Percentage of villages/Harijanwads without link roads	67.00	4.80
12.	Percentage of population covered under Rural Water Supply	66.00	75.00
13.	Per capita plan outlay during VIIth Plan	198.15	1,173.71

The development gap between SCs and general population is estimated as an index at 84.08 (Index Value) by giving positive and negative weights to development indicators and taking the difference between the average weights. The development gap indicates that though SCs have been living in the midst of Hindus and inspite of best opportunities provided to them they are still suffering from certain unfavourable attributes and they are not able to lead the life on par with general population.

As regards the quantitative well being of human life, the income pattern among different social groups is the main indicator. The real per capita income has been the index for deciding the well being of any group. A study in sample villages of Anantapur district reveal that the percentage of distribution of income is 15.82 percent for SCs, 1.10 percent for STs, 36.78 percent for BCs and 46.28 for OCs. Of late there is a marked shift in favour of using a composite set as indices to assess the over-all welfare of population. Non-income aspects of quality life such as large family size, sickness, insufficient food and lack of education and employment besides pessimism, fatalistic parasitic attitude and lack of personal effectiveness etc. are the major factors for assessing the quality of life. The quality of life of SCs is generally associated with illiteracy, ignorance, reliance on traditional norms and overwhelming dependence on fate and environmental factors. Lack of opportunity to education and training to SCs will reduce the potential for vertical mobility in the social system. The factors such as deprivation of children, low level of aspiration, quest for security, low level of political awareness leads to low quality of life. The quality of SCs is to pass through different stages namely awareness, conscientization, interest aggregation, interest organisation and socio-political movements. It realise that politicisation is the only way out for upliftment of the poor SCs. Socially engineered peaceful transition with proper control and planning is the only means today to establish the democratic and egalitarian society without a sharp break from the social and cultural heritage of SCs. An attempt is made hereunder to assess the quality of life for SCs in different sectors of development on the basis of secondary data.

Occupational Pattern

Changes in the traditional occupational structure of SCs have been noticed among certain numerically smallest and larger groups. Some of the Madigas who are traditionally engaged in tanning, leather work and chappal making have now shifted to cultivation, agricultural labour and village servants. Mala Dasus/Mala Dasaries and Mala Jangams who were traditionally religious mendicants and priestly class of Malas are now engaged in cultivation, agricultural labour, handloom and weaving of craise cloth. Bindles who were originally religious functionaries of Madigas have now taken up cultivation as their main occupation. Bygars who were once watchmen of grave-yards are also now seen as cultivators and agricultural labourers. Dom, Dombara, Pindi, Pano, Dondesi, Chalamadi and Mala Sale have also left their traditional occupations and presently engaged in agricultural labour and cultivation. The SCs can be broadly classified into (1) landless agricultural labour communities, (2) artisan or skill specialised groups, (3) communities engaged in leather and allied works, and (4) core groups engaged in scavenging and allied occupations.

Apart from social discrimination, assetlessness and low skill endowment are considered as major causes for acute poverty among SCs resulting in exploitation and low quality of life. Only 17.45 percent of SCs are cultivators and they are mostly small and marginal farmers, share croppers and tenants. Very meagre percentage of SC population is engaged in brick making, mat weaving, stone cutting etc. The low skill endowment of SC population is reflected in secondary and territory sectors such a mining and quarrying (0.6 percent), Household Industry (1.4 percent) other than house-hold industry (2.6 percent) construction (1.3 percent), trade and commerce (1.2 percent), transport storage and communication (2.0 percent) and other services (4.0 percent).

Education and Employment

There are certain appreciable changes in the educational conditions of Scheduled Castes. A significant change in the rate of literacy of SCs from 1.9 in 1931 to 17.65 percent in 1981 is noticed. Educational facilities such as scholarships have also been on increasing trend. About 1.37 lakhs of post-matric scholarships were awarded to SC students in 1991-92 as against 114 scholarships given in 1944-45. Employment poses a serious problem among SCs due to low unskilled nature of their occupations. Most of the illiterates are following traditional occupations. The present situation reveals that non-traditional occupations of higher status though limited in number are in the hands of the educated youth among SCs. The representation of SCs in Government and Public Sector undertakings has been on increasing trend in the State.

TABLE 3
Total No. of Employees as on 1-1-1989

	SCs	*State*	*Ratio*
Class - I	147	3746	0.04—1
Class - II	1,283	23119	0.06—1
Class - III	32,178	268998	0.12—1
Class - IV	31,195	147122	0.21—1
Total	65,580	442995	0.15—1

Though the ratio of employment for the State as a whole appears to be 15 percent, there is a remarkable short-fall of SC employees in Class-I and Class - II services.

Health and Nutrition

The phenomenon of nutritional deficiency, proneness to disease and low productivity are the considered factors for the low quality of life besides the demographic factors like higher rate of infant mortality and large family size. Certain SC families are not able to enjoy the minimum nutrition level consumption due to their peculiar consumption behaviour such as addiction to liquor, gambling, social customs and evils.

The health status of a group depends upon its position in social stratification which is clearly reflected that the deficiency in intake of calories decreases as one moves from the SCs to advanced castes. A study on health status of SCs conducted in Rangampeta village of East Godavari District in 1984 reveals that out of 48 selected households consisting of 227 persons, 80 percent of SC population suffered from some morbidity episodes. Nearly half of the morbidity episodes were concentrated in the age group of 35-54 resulting in loss of earnings to the families, sometimes depriving the family members of the essential items like food, medicine etc. Among youth 40-70 of morbidities were neglected which indicates their lack of health consciousness, lack of affordability of time for treatment for fear of loss of wages, lack of sufficient means for seeking health care etc., 30 percent of the morbidities were ignored completely without taking any health action thereby incapacitating the persons to work and further loss in earnings.

It is observed that malnutrition is noticed among SCs, SC women who suffer from severe malnutrition and ill-health due to high fertility and lower health care facilities. Their participation as farm or wage labourers during pregnancy location and illness worsens their health as well as their children. According to the recent discovery of medical experts, the two simple methods viz., mass immunization and dehydration can remarkably reduce the incidence of infant and child mortality among different social groups. It is estimated that five million children die every year of dehydration. Four million of these children can be saved through a simple method of dehydration. Mass immunization method saves one half the five million children who each year die from a wide variety of diseases.

A dissertation of Dr. B.S. N. Noori presented to the University of Health Science for the award of M.Sc. degree in Applied Nutrition on Nutritional Profile of Rural Pre-school Children Belonging to Harijan Community reveals that morbidity was higher in Harijans except for cunjuctivities. The prevalance of Vitamin-A deficiency and B. Complex deficiency were higher among the Harijans, and non-Harijans as compared as NNMR figure. The extent of moderate and severe degree malnutrition was higher in 1-3 year old children (66-70 percent) than in 3-5 years old (54-56 percent).

Food Consumption

Among 1-3 years SC children the consumption of cereals and millets which was predominantly rice was about 167 grams per day which was only a marginally lower than the recommended level of 175 grams per day. The consumption of protective foods like pulses (3gms), other vegetables (11gms), milk and milk products (92 gms) were much lower than the R.D.A. The consumption of green leafy vegetables was negligible (less than one gram/day) and that of sugar and jaggary was 13 gms. The average consumption of fats and oils was found to be 3 gms/day as against recommended level of 15 gms/day. The consumption pattern of various foodstuffs was found to be similar among 4+ children also.

The average intake of Calories among 1-3 year children was found to be 729 kcal/day against recommended level of 1120 kcal/day. The main intake of protein was found to be 16.1 gms.

against RDA of 22 gms/day. The intake of Calcium (97 mg/day), Iron (7.1 mg/day), Vit.A (95 mg/day), Thiamine (0.28 mg/day), Rihoflavine (0.26 mg/day) were far below the recommended levels. Even among 4 + children the pattern of nutrients intake was observed to be similar.

A dissertation of Dr. Ahiam Salah Bih Briek presented to the University of Health Science for the award of MSc. (Applied Nutrition) on Prevalance of Nutritional Anaemia is quite high in SC population living in rural Hyderabad and the extent is widespread. Among the two known major vulnerable groups the magnitude as well as severity is more in children as compared to women. The survey has indicated that Haemoglobin status showed a clear cut income gradient. Anaemia in the community is mainly of Iron deficiency which can be rectified with Iron rich foods i.e., green leafy vegetables next to cereals in the context of Indian diets. Since the prevalance of anaemia is widespread in young children and women, it is suggested that there is an urgent need to strengthen the implementation of the Anaemia Prophylazis programme.

Infrastructure and Consumption

Housing, it is observed has had an improvement in the types of houses occupied by SCs since IV Five Year Plan. However, in rural areas the houses of SCs are still segregated.

The survey reveals that 9489 SC localities are not having connected roads and 11987 SC localities require repairs. 3500 SC localities are not electrified. No street light arrangements are made in 6384 SC locaiities. The survey also revealed that though street lights are provided in 8172 SC localities, but these are not in working condition. Drainage and sanitation is not given attention in SC localities.

The social tensions in the society are happening in the form of atrocities due to certain changes in the pattern of income and consumption levels and access to resource of these groups.

It is quite evident that agricultural labourers and marginal farmers among SCs are having lowest per capita consumption levels though the process of development has increased the share of wage labour. Monthly per capita expenditure 90 food items (cereals, pulses and edible oils) in rural areas of the State is worked out to be Rs. 45.38.[3]

The quality of life of SC women deserve special attention. They constitute highly vulnerable group from the point of view of their predominance in unskilled casual labour, poor occupational diversification, lower wage rates and higher incidence of unemployment. This situation is further aggravated by the increasing trend of female headed households. The regional and micro-level studies reveal that women get a relatively small share of the total food consumption mainly because of the custom and traditional values. The women headed households besides economic deprivation suffer from social deprivation which ultimately reduced their access to development opportunities.

Problems and Suggestions

The Social Philosophy of Dr. B.R.Ambedkar is animated by the spirit of humanism. His social philosophy emphasizes not merely material progress and spiritual enlightenment but also the alround development of human personality. His programme of humanism is mainly concerned with the emancipation of the poor, the fallen and the weak. He stands for radical and fundamental changes in the traditional way of the Indian people so that "the benefits will not be usurped by the few but will accrue to all." Thus, his programme of social reform is meant for all. Dr. Ambedkar opposed capitalism, dictatorship and totalitarianism. He emphatically stressed that "Democracy must be the governing principle of human relationship based on the fundamental values of liberty, equality and fraternity".[4] The social humanism, the gospel of Dr. Ambedkar aims at securing an integrated human personality as well as an emotionally integrated human society and implies to regard every human being as an end in himself with a right to his own development in his own way.

As regards the development of SCs, the Economists, Planners, Executives, Administrators and Social Practitioners are divided and some of them opined that the development of SCs is a myth. The studies conducted by K.N. Raj (1970), V.M. Dandekar, and Rath, N. (1971), B.S. Minhas (1974), and A.D. Puranik (1974) revealed that "the rich according to them always escaped its ill-effects and the poor fall sad victims throughout the length and breadth of India." Contrary to this Prof. K. Sachidananda (1971) in his report on Studies of SCs with special reference to change (A Trend Report) I.C.S.S.R., New Delhi stated that "the Scheduled Castes have travelled a long way from what they had been about[4] decades go and that there is lot of change in the social economic conditions in all parts of India".

Another group of Economists and Social Scientists specially Srivasthava A.L, H.S.Varma and J.V.Raghavendra Rao (1970) E.V.S Patrudu (1971), R.N Kulahalli and A.Bopegomagi (1972) and Khan, Mumtaz Ali (1980) argued that absence of change among the SCs is a myth, maintain that they have to change a lot still to acquire social and economic equality with the rest of the Indian society.

Dr. Ambedkar, a social revolutionary while demanding reservations and other protective devices, he paid specific attention on basic things like land, education, political power and social reforms to solve the problems of Scheduled Castes. He opined that economic emancipation is the very foundation for the social progress of Scheduled Castes. In the context of Dr. Ambedkar's social philosophy, the programmes and policies for the development of Scheduled Castes are to be moulded to aim at integrated human society. Economic policy has to shift its emphasis from quantity to quality with new technologies and techniques, low cost, improved management, and high efficiency. In a nutshell, to improve the quality of life of SCs, it is essential to mould the economic and social policy by adopting the following measures—

1. Dr. Ambedkar opined that "the low rank of Harijans was derived from cumulative inequalities in the economic, political and ritual systems". The total perception of Ambedkar about the problems of SCs is still relevant and the development gap worked out for SCs and general population indicates that there is still a long way to improve the quality of life of SCs. Heavy investment is needed to reduce the development gap between SCs and general population. Further, balanced approached for investment in human resources in the form of health, education and training is essential which results in higher productivity among the members of Scheduled Castes.

2. It is observed that development benefits are enjoyed by only a section of Scheduled Castes at the cost of rural poor and vulnerable SC masses. In order to safeguard these masses to get their share of development benefit, it would be desirable to allot 80 percent of the 15 percent SC reserved quota to the rural poor and the vulnerable SC masses by classifying the SCs into two classes—(i) those benefited by reservations and (ii) those not benefited by reservations. However, the benefited class will get 20 percent. The process of reservation has to be reviewed for every 10 years.

3. Dr. Ambedkar suggested in 1950s that all waste land in the country would be put in list-I of the Constitution (within the purview of the Union Government) for settling SC people. Land reforms programme should be pushed through with greater vigour. Further as suggested by B.S.Minhas, an integrated programme of consolidation of land holdings with complimentary development works has to be taken up.

4. The primary producer among Weaker Sections especially SCs has to sell his produce at a lesser rate during harvest period and he is forced to purchase the same produce during lean season at a higher rate. To avoid this type of situation it would be advisable to establish grain banks in rural backward areas especially in SC localities. Further there is every need to minimise the gap between procurement rate of producers and the sale price for consumers of different essential commodities.

5. Dr. Ambedkar, a passionate champion of labour unions and legislations, long back realised that Harijans are bound to be wage earners and their interests could be protected through various measures. There are no trade unions in the rural areas for implementation of minimum agriculture wages. Besides, effective implementation of minimum agricultural wages, insurance to agricultural labour, provision of Krishi Centres to children of agricultural labour families, common farm shelters against rain and hot sun, common threshing floors etc., should form part of social policy in a Welfare State.

6. The aim of application of appropriate science and technology is to improve the competitive abilities of the members of weaker sections vis-a-vis the organised sector specially by protection of markets, grant of subsidies and systematic research. The adoption of technology should not be costly, risky

and incapable of management by the targeted groups. As such there is need to evolve some sort of viable technology to take care of social needs especially the "pent up" needs of the Weaker Sections in rural areas considering the availability of resources and population potentiality.

7. Ambedkar opined that education should be open to all on equal terms and without education, they cannot realise the real value of their rights. He stressed that education must be accompanied by Sila and it may not be fruitful to the masses without Sila. Quality education for the weak especially among smaller children population, dependent, widowed, divorced and abandoned women and youth needs concerted and concentrated efforts of State and Central Governments. It is needless to emphasise the human resource development among SCs with emphasis on elimination of social poverty factors, social deprivation, building up inner strength and managerial capabilities. Further, coaching programmes for various competitive examinations and market oriented courses with emphasis on vocational guidance requires specific attention. Women's Integrated Learning for Life (WILL) is one of the fundamental development programmes for improving the quality of life of SC women.

8. Housing for masses is to be made a part of social justice by giving preference to landless and houseless vulnerable groups coupled with employment and improvement in ecology.

9. Safe drinking water in all the SC localities is inevitable as part of minimum needs programme. Sanitation in the SC localities requires urgent attention of authorities.

10. Public distribution system in SC localities needs improvement with regard to supply of essential commodities by exclusively establishing fair price shops for SCs. SC consumers should be protected from the supply of inferior quality goods, shabby goods and adulterated goods. Under P.D.S. supply of essential commodities can be made on "Credit Card" system especially during lean seasons to consumers through Agricultural Cooperative Credit Societies at village level only in drought prone districts and in identified backward pockets of backward districts. Credit worthiness and purchasing power of the SC consumers needs to be strengthened.

11. Unproductive expenditure on items like liquor, toddy should be reduced in order to promote the saving habit among Scheduled Castes.

12. Population explosion among Weaker Sections should be avoided. Two child norm should be socially acceptable.

13. To achieve the spirit of social humanism as enunciated by Dr. B.R. Ambedkar, special efforts are to be made to see that social deprivation and social poverty are things of past and are not found in the present society. Untouchability prone areas are to be identified and social change has to be brought about by social animators and voluntary organisations through peaceful social engineering techniques.

14. As politicisation plays a vital role, in eliminating the social disabilities, one of the important measures is to have balance of control over rural institutions like cooperatives, Panchayat Raj Institutions, youth clubs, women organisations etc. in rural areas.

15. Popular participation of people is a pre-requisite for effective and successful implementation of any development programmes to improve the quality of life.

16. Promotions of mutual understanding, mutual help, constructive cooperation, curtailment on egoism, jealousy and violence are the cardinal principles of peaceful social engineering among different social groups in the society.

References

1. Govt. of A.P., *Draft Eighth Five Year Plan (1990-91)*, Planning Dept, Hyderabad, p. 90.
2. Kopparthy, S.N.M. "Health Status of Scheduled Castes", *Social Change*, Vol. 21, No. 1, March, 1991.
3. *Report on Household Consumer Expenditure* NSS 42nd Round (State Sample), July, 1985 - June, 1987, Directorate of Economic & Statistics, Govt. of A.P., Hyderabad.
4. Janata, D.R., *The Social Philosophy of Dr.Ambedkar*, Phoenix Publishing House, Agra, 1965.

15

Ambedkar in Search of a Lenin—Dilemmas of Dalit Movement

*V. Prasanna Kumar**

Voluminous literature has been generated during this centenary year of Dr. B.R. Ambedkar depicting different facets of his contribution to the toiling Dalits of India in particular and to Indian polity at large. Yet a humble attempt is made in this paper to implode yet another vividity of Ambedkar's thought and contribution in the light of contemporary Indian socio-political context. Thereby, the underlying objective is to enrich 'Ambedkarism' as a more meaningful and objective means of Dalit liberation as a movement that had lost its vigour, focus, sharpness and direction after the demise of its heralder Dr. B.R. Ambedkar and presently which is caught under the deadlock of increasing participation in democratic franchise and yet the perpetuation of slavery, heinous atrocities, arsonage and looting of wealth; physical, moral and biological. There are two ways of looking at Ambedkar— one, as an indomitable social reformer and the other as the law-giver of Independent India. The ongoing analysis would tell us as to how these two tried to contradict and condition each other. Viewed from the first angle, Dr. Ambedkar was comprehensive and uncompromisingly committed to the cause of Dalit emancipation. In addition to this, one can find Ambedkar as very much conditioned and contented as law-giver. It was crystal clear from his own following statement in Rajya Sabha—

---

* Lecturer in Political Science, Indira Gandhi National Open University Regional Centre, Begumpet, Hyderabad-16.

> People always keep on saying to me "Oh, you are the maker of the Constitution". My answer is I was a hack. What I was asked to do, I did much against my will."[1]

This gap in his perceptions and permutations has further widened over time and space during the four decades of constitutional journey and jurisprudence. If these gaps over time and space are not abridged even at this late hour the entire constitutional edifice on which Dr. Ambedkar has relied upon for delivering the goods of Dalit liberation might collapse as a castle of cards to the brink of social divergence.

The reason for a good part of this paralytic state lies in the inability of Dalit organizations and intellectuals to refine, rediscover and reinterpret of what Ambedkar had said and thought to have been the best attainable in consonance with the demands of his times and space. The present disgraceful state of the Dalits is notable with markedly contrasting developments. One is the intravertly growing apathy of the general public and people at the helm of governance to the supposedly prolonged presence of constitutional safeguards to Dalits. On the other side one can witness the complete collapse of Dalit organizations, social and political, in meeting this challenge of apathy with powerful and rationally sound reinterpretations of Ambedkarism.

Dalit organizations must immediately address themselves to this task. Failure of this is bound to jeopardize the constitutional process of Dalit elevation and might place them at the crossroads of wholesome humiliation and peril. Precisely, it is this that differentiates the thought of Ambedkar and that of Marx. Like Marx, to the toiling workers of the world, Ambedkar had not only produced an excellent socio-political philosophy but also the requisite state mechanisms for the peaceful liberation of Indian Dalits. But the only unfortunate difference is that Ambedkar failed to get a heir to hatch over his ideology like Lenin and Mao to Marx. It is in this context that the demand for a potential monolithic national Dalit organization and leadership assumes immediate attention.

I

There are three important aspects of Ambedkar's thought which need to be redressed by all of us in this august assembly— (1) the efficacy of reservations as an instrument of Dalit liberation and why Ambedkar has chosen to exclude defence services from the purview of reservation policy, (2) increasing mockery of political reservations and (3) Does Dalits require a political organization of their own? While attending to these questions we shall first see what Ambedkar had thought on these three areas? How was he constrained and forced to content with and finally what can be done further to make realize the Ambedkarian goal of Dalit emancipation?

II

Article 335 of the Indian Constitution reads like this—

The *Claims* of the members of the Scheduled Castes and Scheduled Tribes shall be taken into consideration, consistently with the *maintenance of the efficiency* of administration in the making of appointments to *services* and posts in connection with the affairs of the Union or of a State.

This is the basic article upon which the reservations for SCs and STs in government jobs is extended. Two things are worth noting in this article. One, there is no time limit attached to this and secondly, the literal meaning of the word 'services'. Indeed, while the Constitutent Assembly was at work, there were demands from some members to prescribe certain time frame for these reservations as was the case with political reservations. However, the scholar, visionist and crusader in Ambedkar succeeded in persuading the assembly to withdraw such demands after explaining that the centuries old backwardness and exploitation cannot be expected to be remedied in a narrow time frame. However, one vitally important sector of governance, viz. the defence services were excluded from the scope of reservations resulting in an unquantifiable loss culturally and educationally to the Dalits apart from economic.

For Ambedkar, education was not simply a means for the development of child's personality or was just a source of earning livelihood. Rather, he considered education as the most powerful agent of mobility and social change. It is an essential prerequisite for launching any social movement, in modern times. For him, education was a vehicle to liberate the Dalits from illiteracy, ignorance and superstitions and thus enable them to fight against all forms of injustice, exploitation and oppression.

Ambedkar advised the Dalits to leave their traditional callings and take up secular occupations which they could achieve only by educating themselves and their children. By receiving education, including technical and professional education, he believed that the Dalits might be able to break the age-old caste-based structure of division of labour in our society. "We may forgo material benefits of civilization, but we cannot forgo our right and opportunity to reap the benefits of the highest education to the fullest extent....Backward Classes have just realized that without education their existence is not safe"[2] remarked Dr. Ambedkar in his speech on the Bombay University Act Amendment Bill in the Bombay Legislative Council on 5th October 1927. It was this statesmanly vision that made Dr. Ambedkar to give the following message to his brethren—"Educate, Organize and Agitate".

Keeping in view the crucial role of education in social emancipation of the Dalits, he submitted on 19 March 1928, a report on the educational advancement of different communities in Bombay Presidency in 1923 to the Indian statutory Commission. The report revealed that although the Brahmins and the allied castes formed the smallest group in respect of the total population, they stood first in order of the level of education. The data were as follows—

Communities	*Order in Respect of Population*	*Order in Respect of Education*
Advanced Hindus (Brahmins and allied castes)	IV	I
Intermediate Hindus (marathas and allied castes)	I	III
Backward Hindus (Depressed Castes and Tribes)	II	IV
Mohammedans	III	II

While the Depressed Classes constituted the second largest group in respect of population, they stood lowest on educational ladder. Thus, it followed that *if the disparity in education was to be removed, it was necessary that these classes should be given pref-*

erential treatment. Dr. Ambedkar remarked that if the Depressed Classes were to be brought to the level of equality with others, *the remedy was to adopt the principle of inequality and to give favoured treatment to those who were below the level of education.*

But what the 40 years history of reservations for SCs and STs in education and employment speak? The statistics are stark and revealing.

TABLE 1

Category	*Literacy Rates*			*Growth Rate*	
	1961	*1971*	*1981*	*1961-71*	*1971-81*
General	24.00	29.45	36.23	22.71	23.02
Scheduled Castes	10.27	14.67	21.38	42.84	45.74
Scheduled Tribes	8.54	11.29	16.35	32.20	44.82
All Communities Excluding SCs and STs	27.91	33.80	41.30	21.10	22.19

Source : Report of the Commissioner for SCs and STs, 1987.

Although the rate of growth of literacy amongst SCs and STs was faster during seventies compared to sixties, yet it is quite slow. The gap in the literacy rate between SCs and STs on the one hand and the other communities has widened notwithstanding the growth of literacy as will be evident from the following figures—

	1961	*1971*	*1981*
Gap between Literacy Rates among the Scheduled Castes and Non-SC/ST Communities	17.64	19.13	19.92
Gap between Literacy Rates among the Scheduled Tribes and Non-SC/ST Communities	19.37	22.51	24.95

It is on the records that still 79.42 percent of SCs and 83.65 percent of ST population remains illiterate. This being the general literacy position of literacy among SC and ST women is still worse.

TABLE 2

Category	*Literacy Rates*		*Growth Rate*
	1971	*1981*	*1971-81*
Scheduled Castes	6.44	10.93	69.72

Category	Literacy Rates		Growth Rate
	1971	1981	1971-81
Scheduled Tribes	4.85	8.04	65.77
All Communities Excluding SCs and STs	22.25	29.43	32.27

Source : Report of the Commissioner for SCs and STs, 1987.

Even after 42 years of constitutional protection, 90 percent of SC women and 92 percent of ST women continue to be illiterates. It is to our common knowledge that a vast majority of School Drop-outs are also from these two communities.

TABLE 3

Category	*Primary Stage Classes I-V*	*Middle Stage Classes VI-VIII*	*Secondary Stage Classes I-X*
SC	59.21	74.76	85.77
ST	74.00	84.99	91.65

Source : Report of the Commissioner for SCs and STs, 1987.

A separate State-wise and country-wise break-up of drop-out rates also is given at Annexure 1. If such is the pathetic position of drop-outs, let us have a look at the enrolment position.

As per the split-up, State-wise and country-wise given at Annexure 2, it is evident that only 7.36 percent of SC students and 1.68 percent of ST students are being enrolled into all undergraduate, post-graduate and professional courses.

Then, to where does all this poor literacy and enrolment levels combined with high drop-out rates lead? *Nowhere but to a large scale de-reservation of reserved vacancies in government sector and towards greater immobilization of these communities of the social mainstream.* Here are some painful statistics with regard to the employment of SCs and STs in Government and allied sectors.

A comparative statement showing the representation of SCs and STs in services under the Central Government, Public Sector Undertakings and Public Sector/Nationalized Banks as on 10 - 10 - 1987.

TABLE 4
Government of India

Group	*Total*	*SC*	*%*	*ST*	*%*
A	57,654	4,746	8.23	1.180	2.05
B	75,419	7,847	10.40	1.447	1.92
C	21,30,453	3,07,980	14.46	90,147	4.23
D(Excluding Sweepers)	11,67,759	2,34,614	20.09	68,206	5.84
Total	34,31,285	5,55,187	16.18	1,60,980	4.69

Public Sector Undertaking (211 PSUS)

A	1,61,825	7,862	4.86	1,904	1.17
B	1,62,339	10,010	6.17	2,522	1.55
C	13,94,015	2,58,500	18,54	1,23,017	8.82
D(Excluding Sweepers)	3,99,000	1,23,010	30.82	68,111	17.07
Total	21,17,179	3,99,382	18.86	1,95,554	9.24
Sweepers	38,900	30,150	77.51	1,311	3.37

Public Sector & Nationalized Banks

Officers	2,15,805	15,745	7.29	3,986	1.84
Clerks	4,49,144	61,891	13.77	16,957	3.77
Subordinate staff	1,67,136	37,272	22.30	7,721	4.61
Total	8,32,085	1,14,908	13.81	28.664	3.44

Source : Report of the Commissioner of SCs and STs, 1987.

The situation of SC and ST employment in the universities, the universal seats of learning and the most vocal support centres of reservation policy is surprisingly still worse.

TABLE 5

Category	*Total*	*SC*	*%age*	*ST*	*%age*
Teaching posts in 41 Universities					
Professors	2,133	13	0.61	1	0.05
Readers/Associate	3,261	34	1.04	5	0.15
Lecturers	5,341	169	3.16	32	0.60

Category	Total	SC	%age	ST	%age
Research Associates, etc.	674	71	10.53	2	0.30
Ministerial posts in 41 Universities					
Group A	3,525	118	3.35	11	0.31
Group B	4,833	221	4.51	48	0.99
Group C	19,811	1,686	8.51	219	1.11
Group D	17,607	2,628	14.93	616	3.50

The momentous and politically motivated special drives are of little solace to the community. All this drives us home to the clear point that reform should start at the grassroot level and not from the periphery. And it is precisely here the need arises in search of new vistas in reservations stemming from the base-level of the socio-economic setting of the SCs and STs. And this search is sure of finding an answer in the *demand for "extension of reservation in defence services"*.

The defence services of India is the fourth largest in the world with a total of 12,60,000 armed personnel (excluding 4,60,000 reserved forces) and also with an annual outlay of 4 to 5 percent of the GNP. On 1951 to 1992 India has spent a total of Rs. 148,501.6 crores on defence. The year-wise break up for which is given as follows—

TABLE 6

Trends in India's Defence Expenditure (1951-92)

Year	*Defence Expt. at Current Prices Rs. In Crores*	*Defence Exp. As % of GNP*	*Defence Exp. As % of Central Govt. Expenditure*
1951-52	181.1	1.8	33.8
1952-53	185.5	1.9	35.6
1953-54	196.5	1.9	33.0
1954-55	195.1	2.0	20.0
1955-56	189.8	1.9	20.8
1956-57	211.8	1.8	19.4
1957–58	279.8	2.4	19.0
1958–59	278.8	2.2	18.9
1959–60	267.0	2.0	13.4
1960–61	280.9	2.0	15.3

Year	*Defence Expt. at Current Prices Rs. In Crores*	*Defence Exp. As % of GNP*	*Defence Exp. As % of Central Govt. Expenditure*
1961–62	312.5	2.1	15.0
1962–63	473.9	3.0	27.0
1963–64	816.1	4.5	32.4
1964–65	805.8	3.8	22.8
1965–66	884.8	4.0	22.6
1966–67	908.5	3.6	19.7
1967–68	968.4	3.3	21.1
1968–69	1033.2	3.4	19.5
1969–70	1100.9	3.3	20.5
1970–71	1199.3	3.3	20.0
1971–72	1525.3	3.9	20.4
1972–73	1652.2	3.8	20.8
1973–74	1680.8	3.1	21.3
1974–75	2112.3	3.3	19.0
1975–76	2472.3	3.7	18.4
1976–77	2562.5	3.6	17.7
1977–78	2633.6	3.3	16.0
1978–79	2867.6	3.3	17.4
1979–80	3355.6	3.5	17.3
1980–81	3866.8	3.4	17.3
1981–82	4651.8	3.6	15.6
1982–83	5408.3	3.7	16.2
1983–84	6309.2	3.7	–
1984–85	6660.5	3.5	–
1985–86	7862.0	4.2	–
1986–87	10194.0	4.7	–
1987–88	12512.0	–	–
1988–89	13237.0	–	–
1989–90	14298.0	–	–
1990–91	15643.0	–	–
1991–92	16227.0	–	–

Source : Report of the Commissioner for SCs and STs, 1987.

By setting aside the defence services from the purview of reservations, to put the argument straight, the SCs and STs of India have no share in the national defence. Above all they are being disgracefully denied of their rightful duty of defending the nation in times of peril. Their rightful entry into services on reservation is being dubbed as a compromise with India's defence preparedness and its capabilities. It is also whispered, it may even communalise the Indian army.

A deeper analysis would suggest both these arguments as just cannons. What does the social history of Dalits reveal? These are highly illiterate, insecure, innocent, foolish, segregated and slavish mobs whose life is nothing but day to day struggle for bread and butter, struggle against oppression and exploitation.

TABLE 7
Crimes against SCs and STs during 1986

Nature of Crime	*Against SC*	*Against ST*
Murder	564	160
Grievous hurt	1,408	311
Rape	727	285
Arson	1,002	232
Other offences	11,715	2,957
Total	15,416	3,945

Source : Report of the Commissioner for SCs and STs, 1987.

What does this gruesome crime chart reveal? That struggle for dignity, equity, basic needs and survival has been their daily bread. And in the course of these perilously perennial struggles they have turned out to be the real warriors of self-protection. What does the history of Indian political parties speak? You take the criminal records, you observe the political riots, you scan the fractional wars both inter-party and intra-party. Where from the political parties drew their henchmen? Who are the loyal bodyguards for the caste Hindu political leaders? Are they not mostly from Dalit communities? If such is the proven socio-criminal record of these sections, are they not fit for or courageous enough to fight for the nation? Let they be allowed to sacrifice for the nation instead for their feudal political lords. Then what is the real problem? The real problem seems only to be if the Dalits start joining the army on a large scale on reservations and start fortifying the Indian defences, the political parties might in the longrun may have to be wary of their own defence.

Let us answer to the communal question. To begin with, can anyone affirm that the present Indian defence organization is non-communal? Can we forget that we are just continuing the British legacy of communal defence? Is it not a fact that the very basis of our defence organisation is still communal competition of servitude? Otherwise why is there the Jat regiment, the Rajput regiment, the Sikh regiment, Maratha regiment, Gorkha regiment etc? Yet the SCs and STs are not demanding a Dalit regiment of their own. Is it not a fact that in the barracks provision is made for the erection of temples, churches and Gurudwaras but not Masjids? Does the Dalits entry into military with reservation make it more communal that what it is today?

The nodal point here is how best the Indian defence services can be made use of in the social, cultural and economic emancipation of Dalits? The defence services do have the mighty potential of *setting right the individual from a state of anarchy to discipline which the Dalits in India are precisely in need of.* Secondly, it assures fixed monthly economic returns not only to the individual but also to his parents or other dependents. Instead of pouring lakhs of crores of rupees on poverty alleviation programmes on which the financial returns are always doubtful and debatable, *it is fruitful for one person from every illiterate SC and ST family must be recruited in to the army.* Thirdly, while serving the army these people not only get exposed to different cultures of vast and porous India, but can be brought out of the age old avail of social segregation. Finally, with all this, and by utilizing the best available educational services in the military and other central schools, *there is bound to be a generational leap in the social, economic, educational and cultural outfit of SCs and STs.*

All this is part of social elevation process for which Ambedkar devoted himself to.

Ambedkar believed that social freedom should go hand in hand with political freedom. In his words, "Political power cannot be a panacea for all the ills of the Depressed Classses. Their salvation lies in their social elevation. They must clean their evil habits. They must improve their bad ways of living. *By a change in their mode of life they must be made fit for respect and friendship.* They must be educated. There is a great necessity to disturb their pathetic contentment and to instil into them that divine discontent which is the spring of all elevation".[3]

This job of change in culture, approach and outlook and the infusion of self-confidence and self-motivation can be performed best by the defence services. Though Ambedkar was fully aware of the vast potentials of Indian defence organization, he was constrained and made to content with what it is, in view of the then going debate of a need for secular army in the wake of partition. And it was justified on his part but it is now high time for us to address ourselves to this unfinished task and to make a search for the correct interpretation of the words *services and posts* under the Union as read in article 335 which might include even the defence services.

III

It is an irony of history that Dr. Babasaheb Ambedkar was defeated in the elections to Parliament (Lok Sabha) from reserved seats in Bombay and Bhandara in 1952 and 1954, respectively, at the hands of obscure Scheduled Caste candidates sponsored by the Congress Party. There is no gain saying the fact that Babasaheb was a towering figure and a political giant of incomparable stature. He was the main architect of the Indian Constitution. A highly qualified man with an impressive array of academic degrees, a barrister of repute, a great orator and a political leader of the first order. Dr. Ambedkar will be remembered more as a social revolutionary who worked ceaselessly in the service of the Scheduled Castes and Tribes. And yet he was defeated by persons who were non-entities as compared to him. Dr. Ambedkar's defeat demonstrated, unmistakably, that political reservation is a great impediment in the way of real representatives of the weaker sections getting elected to the legislatures. The party bosses see to it that the real champions of the down-trodden are defeated by their own 'show-boys'.

If the leaders of the national political parties of India do honestly feel that political reservation is a genuine historical necessity for the Scheduled Castes and Tribes, then they should take the necessary steps to ensure that only those with a proven record of service to these weaker sections are nominated by them as candidates. In the ultimate analysis, this would be possible only if the Scheduled Castes and Tribes voters alone are given the right to vote in the reserved constituencies. Thereby the contestants in reserved constituencies will be liberated from the clutches of money power, muscle power and from the domination and dictates of the upper castes.

Reservation in the Parliament and State Legislatures provided for the Scheduled Castes and Scheduled Tribes through Articles 330 and 332 of the Constitution was initially to remain operative for a period of 10 years. Article 334 provided this 10 years duration which has been extended four times since 1960 when it first expired. The very fact that this deadline for political reservation for the Scheduled Castes and Tribes has to be extended four times shows that there is something basically wrong with this system of reservation which has failed to achieve its objective even after four decades. The plight of these sections of society has further worsened and their problems have remained largely unsolved. What is worse, most of the representatives of the Scheduled Castes and Tribes who got elected on reserved seats have seldom raised their voice in the Parliament and the State Legislatures against the ever increasing atrocities on these Weaker Sections of society. In many cases the representatives of the Scheduled Castes and Tribes elected on reserved seats are virtually the hand-picked nominees of the dominant classes and are subservient to them. Time has, therefore, come when the entire question of political reservation is re-examined with an open mind. Perhaps, *it would be better to go in for double member constituencies with the Scheduled Caste and Scheduled Tribe voters having two votes, one each for both the general and reserved seats and the non SC and ST voters exercising their franchise for the general seats only.* This will enable the Scheduled Castes to elect their real representatives independently without interference from the dominant classes.

As a matter of fact, Ambedkar himself was not happy with the way in which shape the Constitution has come out. In the course of his memorable speech in the Constituent Assembly on 25 November, 1949, he said, "I came into the Constituent Assembly with no greater aspiration than to safeguard the interest of the Scheduled Castes."[4] The same Ambedkar in his historic speech in the Constituent Assembly on the adoption of Constitution motion said—

"On the 26th January 1950, we are going to enter into a life of contradictions. In politics we will have equality and social-contradictions. In politics we will have inequality. In politics we will be recognizing the principle of one man one vote and one vote one value. In our social and economic life, we shall, by reason of our social and economic structure, continue to deny the principle of one man one value. How long shall we continue to live this life of contradictions? How long shall we continue to deny equality in our social and economic life? If we continue to deny it for long, we will do so only by putting our political democracy in peril. We must remove this contradiction at the earliest possible moment or else those who suffer from inequality will blow up the structure of political democracy which this Assembly has so laboriously built up".[5]

And this is what I mean by the gap in Ambedkar's own confessions and conditions. The ill famous Poona pact is yet another illustration of the extreme constraints under which Ambedkar was to act and decide seldom against his own confessions. Dr. Ambedkar forcefully pleaded for according an independent status to the Scheduled Castes at the Round Table Conference in London in 1930-31. His underlying idea being that those who were socially segregated must be politically segregated. And the British Government had acceded to his demand through the Communal Award. Yet being a true patriot he retraced his steps and signed the Poona pact in 1932 with Mahatma Gandhi, voluntarily giving up the demand for separate electorates. "There was before me a duty, which I owed as part of the common humanity to save Gandhi from sure death. I responded to the call of humanity and saved the life of Gandhi by agreeing to alter the Communal Award in a manner satisfactory to Mr. Gandhi".[6] This is just an instance of the conditionality of Ambedkar against his will and faith. As a consequence of these continued conditionings, one should remember that Ambedker died as a frustrated man.

Then, is there any alternative to this conditionality of thought Ambedkar did assign a high profile to social liberation struggles, he never underplayed political struggle. He in fact tried to supplement it to the social struggles. This can be seen evidently in the formation of Independent Labour Party in 1936 and All India Scheduled Castes Federation. Dr. Ambedkar contested the first General Elections in 1952, but he lost. The same year he was elected to the Council of States. Again, in order to enter the House of People, Dr. Ambedkar contested a by-election in 1954, which too he lost. He however, continued to be a member of Council of States. From 1952 till his death in 1956, he virtually functioned as the leader of the Opposition in the Council of States where he displayed his parliamentary and debating skills with consummate case.

After resigning from the Cabinet in 1951, Dr. Ambedkar was a disillusioned man. The failure to get the Hindu Code passed, on which he had set his heart, was a great set-back for him. There were other political developments in the country which were not to his liking. He disliked many of the policies of the Government. In some cases he became a bitter critic of Prime Minister Jawaharlal Nehru and his Government. In this process he even persuaded 3 MPS who were his followers to join the Krishikar Lok Party led by N.G. Ranga.

All this only demonstrates how perplexed and frustrated Ambedkar was towards his last stage. During a heated debate in Rajya Sabha, Ambedkar once bursted in emotion by saying—

> "Sir, my friends tell me that I have made the Constitution. But I am quite prepared to say that I shall be the first person to burn it out. I do not want it. It does not suit anybody."[7]

The richest tribute, we can pay for Ambedkar is to continue these unfinished constitutional struggles with devotion and dedication. And this will be possible *only through a radical monolithic Dalit political organisation at the national level.* Can it happen?

The Republican Party of India which inherited Ambedkar's ideology had made a good beginning but soon collapsed as a result of internal bickerings. Now the community for which Ambedkar had vowed his life is amidst great dangers inter alia disunity being the foremost. No single Dalit organisation presently in India commands national statures. Most of them are regional and even sub-regional. The SC and ST legislators reaping the benefits of reservation are mere prisoners of party discipline. All this only necessitates a non-political Dalit national organisation of its own to butress further the ideological struggles Ambedkar had left behind us. And for this the Dalits are in need of a Lenin or Mao from within their ranks.

References

1. Rajya Sabha Debates, 2 September 1953, col. 874.
2. Shahare, M.L., Dr. B.R. Ambedkar: An Emminent Educationalist: in *Dr. B.R. Ambedkar. The Man and His Message*, Printice Hall of India, New Delhi, 1991, p.135.
3. Mouli, V.R.Chandra, B.R.Ambedkar : Man and His Visions, Sterling Publishers, New Delhi, p.51.
4. Constituent Assembly Debates, 25 November 1949, pp. 973-74.
5. Rajya Sabha Debates, 2 September 1953, col. 877.
6. Keer, Dhananjay, Dr. Ambedkar : Life and Mission, Popular Prakashan, Bombay, 1990. p.194.
7. Rajya Sabha Debates, 2 September 1953, col. 877.

16

Ambedkar on Education

*V.Lalini**

Dr. B.R. Ambedkar's ideas on education are clearly articulated in his early writings and speeches. Dr. Ambedkar, after entering the Bombay Legislative Council in 1927, reacted vehemently against the governmental policies and practices in the field of education. His efforts and contributions for the development of the educational system of Bombay Presidency are highly creative and laudable. Dr. Ambedkar pointed out the inherent contradictions and loopholes in the Colonial system of education. His ideas and reactions were primarily derived from his social and political philosophy.[1] His voluminous writings uncovered the historical roots of the existing inequalities in the Indian society. His consideration of caste as one of the primary 'units' of Social Understanding and Analysis generated certain important methodological issues, which have a significant bearing on the other dimensions of Indian Social Reality.[2] For Ambedkar, educational enterprise is not an isolated and independent system from the over-all social reality. He believed that the nature of educational system and its growth is essentially determined by the underlying rigid structures of the society. According to him, the pattern of inequalities existing in a particular society reflect in its educational practices and institutional structures. Ambedkar considered *history* and *culture* as one of the essential aspects of an educational enterprise. In other words, he had taken into consideration the dynamics of Indian society in explaining the existing Brahmanical and Colonial pedagogical practices and educational policies. This is very clearly evident from his speeches, which lay bare the pseudo-democratic nations of British Raj, whose aim is first to perpetuate the inequalities further and exploit the country culturally, socially and economically.

---

* Reader, College of Education, Osmania University, Hyderabad - 7.

The two important factors which shaped Ambedkar's ideas on education are—[3]

1. His intensive and indepth study of Indian history and cultural tradition.
2. His exposure to the Western Social Philosophies and Democratic ideals during his stay in Europe and United States.

This paper is an attempt to understand Ambedkar's ideas on education from his socio-political and philosophical framework.

According to Dr. Ambedkar, strengthening of primary education is the key for the establishment of social justice. He derived his ideas on education from his social frame of reference, where Equality, Democracy, Liberty, Social justice form the hard core. He emphasized that primary education is very much essential to uplift the children of down-trodden and backward classes. Ambedkar stressed the need to increase the budget of primary education. He says, "I therefore request...to spend more money on primary education, if for nothing else at least for the purpose of seeing that what he spends bears some fruit ultimately."[4] He expressed his agony on the failure of primary education in India under the British rule. The phenomenal wastage and stagnation in primary system shook Ambedkar. He was very critical about the Colonial bureaucratic practices in education. He says that "the object of primary education is to see that every child that enters the portals of a primary school does leave it only at a stage when it becomes literate and continues to be literate throughout the rest of his life"[5]

Ambedkar has given a very high priority to the achievement of the social objectives of education and criticised the government for its meaningless and mechanistic spending on primary education. He also emphasized on the responsibilities of the State to see every child to enter into a school and continue his or her education.

Dr. Ambedkar opposed the Colonial education system which was based on the principles of commercialisation of education.[6] He felt that such kind of practice further perpetuated the inequalities in the society. According to him, "education is different from other institutions," "the purpose of which is to moralise and socialise the people."[7]

As it is primarily concerned with making people into human beings so it should be easily accessible to every one. He also observes the way the commercialisation of education in India, by the Western rulers, gradually sidelined the majority of population, who are down-trodden and backward. In this connection, it is important to note the remarks made by him. Ambedkar says, "Education is something which ought to be brought with in the reach of every one. Education department is not a department which can be treated on the basis of quid pro quo. Education ought to be cheapened in all possible ways and to the greatest possible extent."[8]

Ambedkar criticised the existing system of education and its *principle of favoured treatment* to certain communities. He revealed the nature of the existing anomalies in the education system by taking the total population of different communities and classes. He argued that the Colonial practices are not only strengthening the existing inequalities but also dividing the society into different rigid segments whose differences are highly incommensurable. He thought that the Mohammedan community though less in number compared to the backward intermediate classes is getting more favour from the Colonial rulers.

Ambedkar with his secular outlook objectively assessed the educational performance of various communities. He points out the importance of treating all communities equally in terms of education. For him equal treatment means adopting the principle of inequality and to give favoured treatment to those who are below the level. In other words, inequal treatment is very much necessary since certain communities are highly deviated from the mainstream and are very poor in terms of social and economic power. In this connection Ambedkar says, "I must here emphasize that this country is composed of different communities. All these communities are all equal in their status and progress. If they are to be brought to the level of equality then the only remedy is to adopt the principle of inequality and to give favoured treatment to those who are below the level."[9] Further, he stressed the need for providing special attention and treatment to the backward classes.[10] He was very critical about the British policies in Bombay Presidency, which totally neglected the backward classes. He says, "My only complaint is that government has not yet thought fit to apply this principle to Backward Classes. Economically speaking and socially speaking, backward classes are handicapped in a manner in which no other community is handicapped. I, therefore, think that the principle of favoured treatment must be adopted in their case. As I have shown, their position is worse than that of the Mohamnmedans and my only pleading is that if the most favoured treatment is to be given to those who deserve it and need it most, then the backward classes deserve more attention of Government than do the Mohammedans."[11]

In Bombay Presidency, during the last part of 1920s, the British rulers transferred education from the Council to the local bodies.[12] The constitution of local bodies is highly heterogeneous. The representation from the backward classes which constitute more than half of the population is less than 10 percent. Ambedkar criticised this move on the basis of the following aspects—

1. The members of the local bodies are not totally aware of the necessity and importance of education. He says, "The members of local boards are too uneducated to realise that education is a necessity. Therefore, I say, this council has done great wrong in transfering the responsibilities of education to the hands of those who do not feel for education."[13]

2. Secondly, he argued that the revenues available for local bodies is very much meagre to spend on education. He thought that education should be under the control of the council which is in a sufficient position to spend on education. He believed that the move to transfer of education to the local bodies is to postphone the spread of education among the masses.

3. Thirdly, according to him, the power structure in local bodies are in tune with the interests of the upper caste and classes. Hence, he expressed his fear regarding the biased decision making of the local bodies, which totally neglected the inerests of the private sections. He argued that in order to spread education to the masses, it is very much necessary to have representatives who are enlightened and share the aspirations and desires of the deprived sections.[14] While explaining

the importance of the representation of backward classes, Ambedkar says, "...The deprived classes find themselves in a most helpless condition. They are surrounded by people who by no means share their aspirations or their desires for advancement and betterment. There is, therefore, all the greater necessity. I say that this government should employ certain inspecting agency under their direct control which will see that the depressed classes are not neglected by the bodies to whose charge such an important subject like education has been entrusted."[15]

Ambedkar gave a very high priority to the economic aspects of the system of education. He unearthed the large-scale wastage of money spent on primary education and also criticised the various governmental departments under the colonial rule which were working at cross purposes. In this connection he very interestingly explains the institutional practices of the Department of Education and the Department of Excise in Bombay Presidency. He says, "I think it is only fair that our educational expenditure should be so adjusted that we should spend on the education of the people as much as we take from them in the form of excise".[16]

Ambedkar recommended scholarships and financial assistance for the children coming from deprived communities.[17] He felt that "scholarships as an aid is better than no aid at all".[18] But he is very critical about the method of providing scholarships. He believed that the parents of the deprived children are too ignorant to understand the help given by the government. They consider the scholarships given as family package or aids to meet their expenses. Due to this reason the financial assistance extended to the children of deprived communities is not in a position to meet the educational needs of the child. Though Ambedkar explained the failure of the method of giving scholarships to the deprived children but his argument is very weak in explicating the socio-economic basis of their facilities.[19] In other words, it is not just the ignorance of the parents but primarily the existential condition of necessities, economic needs and poverty made them to consider children's scholarships as financial aids. No doubt that Dr. Ambedkar acknowledged the complete network and multiple reasons which play in the environment of deprived children. But his explanation skipped certain important dimensions of social reality which essentially shaped the deprived classes. Ambedkar felt that rather than financial assistance, promoting hostels and providing other necessary infra-structure and environment is very much essential for promoting the education of the backward classes.

References

1. Rajasekharaia, A.M., 1987, *Social Philosophy of Dr. B.R. Ambedkar*, Dr. B.R. Ambedkar Memorial Trust, Hyderbad p. 2-3
2. *Ibid.*, pp. 6-7.
3. Mouli Chandra V. 1990, *B.R. Ambedkar - Man and His Vision*, Sterling Publisher Pvt. Ltd., New Delhi.
4. Ambedkar B.R. (1927), On Grants For Education in *Dr. Baba Saheb Ambedkar, "Writings and speches" Vol.2*, Edited by Vasant Moon, Education Department, Government of Maharashtra, Bombay, 1982, p.40.
5. *Ibid.*
6. Kuber W.N : 1991, *Ambedkar - A Critical Study*, People's Publishing House, New Delhi, p. 242..
7. Ambedkar B.R. (1927) : *op. cit.*, p. 39.
8. Ambedkar B.R. (1927) : *op. cit.*, pp. 40-41.
9. Ambedkar B.R. (1927) : *op. cit.*, p. 42
10. Bakshi, S.R : 1992, *B.R. Ambedkar - Statesman and Constitutionalist*, Anmol Publications, New Delhi, p. 74.
11. Ambedkar B.R. (1927) : *op. cit.*, p. 42.
12. Kuber, W.N. *op. cit.*, p. 241.
13. Ambedkar, B.R. (1927) : *op. cit.*, p.43.
14. Kuber, W.N. *op. cit.*, p. 243.
15. Ambedkar, B.R. (1927) : *op. cit.*, p.43.
16. Ambedkar, B.R. (1927) : *op. cit.*, p.40.
17. Kuber, W.N. *op. cit.*, pp. 243244.
18. Ambedkar, B.R. (1927) : *op. cit.*, p. 44.
19. Bakshi, S.R. : *op. cit.*

Annexures

Annexure—I

Drop-out Rates of Scheduled Caste Students 1981-82

Sl. No.	*State/U.T.*	*Primary Stage Classes I-V*			*Middle Stage Classes VI-VIII*	*Secondary Stage Classes I-X*
		Boys	*Girls*	*Total*	*Total*	*Total*
1	2	3	4	5	6	7
	States					
1.	Andhra Pradesh	63.14	68.17	65.14	81.86	85.91
2.	Assam	56.96	61.76	58.93	78.99	69.80
3.	Bihar	70.38	77.70	72.07	83.01	89.92
4.	Gujarat	55.18	61.09	5.47	67.06	75.51
5.	Haryana	23.50	40.52	28.12	57.37	78.89
6.	Himachal Pradesh	28.98	29.29	29.10	55.46	80.91
7.	Jammu & Kashmir	51.77	45.91	49.84	69.09	79.35
8.	Karnataka	67.83	75.12	70.99	71.17	88.77
9.	Kerala	0.0	0.0	0.0	23.71	49.80
10.	Madhya Pradesh	51.91	66.83	56.13	69.13	92.99
11.	Maharashtra	54.89	68.02	60.50	67.86	78.61
12.	Manipur	89.44	91.52	90.45	88.81	83.00
13.	Maghalaya	75.63	63.38	70.69	84.25	86.73
14.	Nagaland	–	–	–	–	–
15.	Orissa	69.53	77.27	72.37	90.71	93.80
16.	Punjab	69.08	76.57	72.53	68.84	84.46
17.	Rajasthan	63.60	77.86	65.74	78.88	83.14
18.	Sikkim	66.97	67.02	66.99	-	-
19.	Tamil Nadu	32.53	45.88	38.54	72.55	84.99
20.	Tripura	61.10	63.60	62.61	83.80	92.04
21.	Uttar Pradsh	44.88	59.50	48.33	76.98	86.95
22.	West Bengal	74.36	78.41	75.72	83.95	91.81

Cont.

Sl. No.	State/U.T.	Primary Stage Classes I-V			Middle Stage Classes VI-VIII	Secondary Stage Classes I-X
		Boys	Girls	Total	Total	Total
	UNION TERRITORIES					
23.	A & N Islands	-	-	-	-	-
24.	Arunachal Pradesh	93.51	96.07	94.42	-	-
25.	Chandigarh	0.0	0.0	0.0	0.0	70.69
26.	D & N Haveli	28.12	47.94	38.68	71.42	91.56
27.	Delhi	32.58	55.68	42.63	62.99	51.10
28.	Goa, Daman & Dui	42.47	47.25	44.43	69.27	81.93
29.	Lakshadweep	-	-	-	-	-
30.	Mizoram	-	-	-	-	-
31.	Pondicherry	1.38	27.89	14.17	63.26	83.68
	Total	56.43	64.24	59.21	74.76	85.72

Source : Report of the Commissioner for SCs and STs, 1987.

Annexure—II

Statewise Enrolment Figures for SC and ST Students at all Under-graduate, Post-graduate, Professional and Technical Courses during 1978-79

Sl.No.	State/U.T.	GRADUATE + POSTGRADUATE COURSES				
		Total	SC	%Age Total	ST	%Age Total
1	2	3	4	5	6	7
	States					
1.	Andhra Pradesh	1,36,490	11,595	8.64	1,306	0.97
2.	Assam	46,703	1,859	4.81	1,570	4.66
3.	Bihar	1,25,679	4,270	3.57	6.425	5.37
4.	Gujarat	1,69,546	10,692	6.31	5,556	3.28
5.	Haryana	58,723	3,217	5.48	33	0.06
6.	Himachal Pradesh	11,118	541	4.87	232	2.09
7.	Jammu & Kashmir	18,087	203	1.14	1	0.01

Sl.No.	State/U.T.	GRADUATE + POSTGRADUATE COURSES				
•		Total	SC	%Age Total	ST	%Age Total
1	2	3	4	5	6	7
	States					
8.	Karnataka	1,71,878	10,624	6.18	1,816	1.06
9.	Kerala	1,93,901	11,396	5.94	6.500	3.39
10.	Madhya Pradesh	1,93,901	11,936	5.94	6,500	3.39
11.	Maharashtra	3,24,704	27,624	8.81	5,699	1.82
12.	Manipur	6,140	36	0.62	334	5.78
13.	Maghalaya	4,879	145	2.98	2,504	51.39
14.	Nagaland	830	–	–	680	81.93
15.	Orissa	45,798	1,432	3.13	866	1.89
16.	Punjab	1,34,996	4,903	4.39	3,001	2.68
17.	Rajasthan	1,34,906	4,903	4,39	3,001	2.68
18.	Sikkim	102	–	–	–	–
19.	Tamil Nadu	1,62,285	12,357	7.62	201	0.12
20.	Tripura	4,458	312	7.10	285	6.39
21.	Uttar Pradesh	4,06,747	44,232	11.46	988	0.26
22.	West Bengal	2,29,155	17,708	8.29	1,396	0.65
	Union Territories					
23.	A & N Islands	416	–	–	13	3.10
24.	Arunachal Pradesh	222	–	–	171	77.03
25.	Chandigarh	15,397	744	4.83	117	0.76
26.	D & N Haveli	–	–	–	–	–
27.	Delhi	74,291	3,621	4.88	164	0.22
28.	Goa, Daman & Diu	6,928	32	0.46	118	0.16
29.	Lakshadweep	–	–	–	–	–
30.	Mizoram	835	8	0.96	713	85.39
31.	Pondicherry	2,485	96	3.86	–	–
	Total	29,43,449	1,80,058	7.36	41,082	1.68

Source : Report of the Commissioner for SCs and STs, 1987.

Annexure—III

Comparative Statement Showing the Representation of the Scheduled Castes and Scheduled Tribes in Services Under the Central Govt. as on 1-1-1977 and 1-1-1987

As on 1-1-1977

Group	*Total strength including SCs & STs*	*Sch. Castes No.*	*Sch. Castes %age*	*Sch. Tribes No.*	*Sch. Tribes %age*
A	39,908	1,662	4:16	309	0.77
B	56,322	3,421	6.07	434	0.77
C	16,77,256	98,662	11.84	46,603	2.78
D(excluding sweepers)	12,46,464	2,37,718	19.07	54,206	4.35
As on 1–1–1977					
A	57,654	4,746	8.23	1,180	2.05
B	75,419	7,847	10.40	1,447	1.92
C	21,30,453	3,07,980	14.46	90,147	4.23
D(excluding sweepers)	11,67,759	2,34,614	20.09	68,206	5.84

Source : Report of the Commissioner for SCs and STs, 1987

INDEX